Long Island can be a great place to hike with your dog. Within a short drive your canine adventurer can be climbing seaside dunes that leave him panting, trotting in rolling pinelands, exploring the estates of America's wealthiest families or circling lakes for miles and never lose sight of the water.

I have selected what I consider to be the 30 best places to take your dog for an outing on Long Island and ranked them according to subjective criteria including the variety of hikes available, opportunities for canine swimming and pleasure of the walks. The rankings include a mix of parks that feature long walks and parks that contain short walks. Did I miss your favorite? Let us know at *www.hikewithyourdog. com.*

For dog owners it is important to realize that not all parks are open to our best trail companions (see page 20 for a list of major parks that do not allow dogs). It is sometimes hard to believe but not everyone loves dogs. We are, in fact, in the minority when compared with our non-dog owning neighbors.

So when visiting a park always keep your dog under control and clean up any messes and we can all expect our great parks to remain open to our dogs. And maybe some others will see the light as well. *Remember, every time you go out with your dog you are an ambassador for all dog owners.*

Grab that leash and hit the trail!
DBG

Doggin' Long Island

The 30 Best Places
To Hike With Your Dog
In New York's Playground

DOUG GELBERT

illustrations by

ANDREW CHESWORTH

Cruden Bay Books

There is always a new trail to look forward to...

DOGGIN' LONG ISLAND: THE 30 BEST PLACES TO HIKE
WITH YOUR DOG IN NEW YORK'S PLAYGROUND

Cruden Bay Books
PO Box 467
Montchanin, DE 19710
www.hikewithyourdog.com

International Standard Book Number 978-0-9815346-3-3

*"Dogs are our link to paradise...to sit with a dog on a hillside
on a glorious afternoon is to be back in Eden,
where doing nothing was not boring - it was peace."*
- Milan Kundera

Ahead On The Trail

Hiking With Your Dog

So you want to start hiking with your dog. Hiking with your dog can be a fascinating way to explore Long Island from a canine perspective. Some things to consider:

🐾 Dog's Health

Hiking can be a wonderful preventative for any number of physical and behavioral disorders. One in every three dogs is overweight and running up trails and leaping through streams is great exercise to help keep pounds off. Hiking can also relieve boredom in a dog's routine and calm dogs prone to destructive habits. And hiking with your dog strengthens the overall owner/dog bond.

🐾 Breed of Dog

All dogs enjoy the new scents and sights of a trail. But some dogs are better suited to hiking than others. If you don't as yet have a hiking companion, select a breed that matches your interests. Do you look forward to an entire afternoon's hiking? You'll need a dog bred to keep up with such a pace, such as a retriever or a spaniel. Is a half-hour enough walking for you? It may not be for an energetic dog like a border collie. If you already have a hiking friend, tailor your plans to his abilities.

🐾 Conditioning

Just like humans, dogs need to be acclimated to the task at hand. An inactive dog cannot be expected to bounce from the easy chair in the den to complete a 3-hour hike. You must also be physically able to restrain your dog if confronted with distractions on the trail (like a scampering squirrel or a pack of joggers). Have your dog checked by a veterinarian before significantly increasing his activity level.

🐾 Weather

Hot, humid Long Island summers do not do dogs any favors. With no sweat glands and only panting available to disperse body heat, dogs are more susceptible to heat stroke than we are. Unusually rapid panting and/or a bright red tongue are signs of heat exhaustion in your pet. Always carry enough water for your hike. Even the prime hiking days of late fall through early spring that don't seem too warm can cause discomfort in dark-coated dogs if the sun is shining brightly. During cold snaps, short-coated breeds may require additional attention.

🐾 Trail Hazards

Dogs won't get poison ivy but they can transfer it to you. Some trails are littered with small pieces of broken glass that can slice a dog's paws. Nasty thorns can also blanket trails that we in shoes may never notice. At the beach beware of sand spurs that can often be present in scrubby, sandy areas.

🐾 Rattlesnakes and Cooperheads

It is at this point in these guides that we warn about the potential dangers of rattlesnakes and other copperheads. Rattlesnakes or copperheads are present in every state; New York State even had a bounty on timber rattlesnakes as late as 1971. But it has been 100 years since a rattlesnake has been seen in the wild east of New York City. In fact, there are no poisonous snakes on Long Island. Your dog may still startle a big snake on the trail, an eastern hognose that was once so common children collected them in buckets to sell to pet stores or a black racer, but nothing to elicit concern.

❧ Black Bears and Coyotes

And even though black bear populations are expanding across the Northeast, Long Island is still not a place they live. Coyotes have also become more common, now living everywhere in New York - except Long Island.

❧ Porcupines

The docile porcupine is slow-moving and easy to catch. Wouldn't you be too if you were covered with a coast of sharp quills? The porcupine is actually a rodent, the world's fourth largest. It is a good climber and is found in forest across temperate climates throughout America.

A balled-up porcupine is a magnet for a curious dog. And a disaster in the waiting if he catches one. If your dog gets quilled try to pull out the sharp quills with whatever tool is available (if you are near home or car, a pair of pliers is your best bet). If you cannot extricate the quill, do not cut it. When cut, the barbed portion of the quill imbedded under the skin is likely to swell, making complete removal extremely difficult.

If you cannot get the quill out, seek professional help as quickly as possible. Try and prevent your dog from rubbing the affected area as this will push the quills in deeper. Easier said than done. The veterinarian will probably anesthesize your dog to accomplish the taks and treat the wound with anti-biotics. Like any trail hazard the best solution is prevention - keep your dog in sight and under control.

❧ Water

Surface water, including fast-flowing streams, is likely to be infested with a microscopic protozoa called *Giardia*, waiting to wreak havoc on a dog's intestinal system. The most common symptom is crippling diarrhea. Algae, pollutants and contaminants can all be in streams, ponds and puddles. If possible, carry fresh water for your dog on the trail - your dog can even learn to drink happily from a squirt bottle.

At the beach, cool sea water will be tempting for your dog but try to limit any drinking as much as possible. Again, have plenty of fresh water available for your dog to drink instead.

Let's Talk Ticks

You could hike with your dog forever on Long Island and never be bothered by ticks. All you need to do is hike only on wide, well-mown and maintained trails and keep your dog squarely in the middle of the path the entire time. But that isn't realistic. So you and your dog are going to pick up ticks while hiking Long Island trails. Let's look at some myths and misconceptions concerning ticks:

TALL TICK TALE #1 - *Removing Ticks From Your Dog (or yourself)*

How many times have you heard that the proper method - the ONLY safe way to remove ticks - is with tweezers. Smearing vaseline on the tick first is even better. This is supposed to guarantee the tick's head will not stay embedded in your dog. Well, how many times do you have vaseline and tweezers at the ready when you find a tick on your dog? The ONLY safe way to deal with a tick is to get it off as quickly as possible. A tick (and we're talking deer ticks, not the larger and much more common dog tick) cannot infect your dog with Lyme Disease bacteria until it is embedded for some time (usually more than 24 hours). So don't be shy about removing a tick with your fingers. Get in there and get it out.

TALL TICK TALE #2 - *Leave As Little Of Your Skin Exposed As Possible To Keep Ticks Off You*

It doesn't take many trips into the woods to realize that wearing long sleeves and tucking long pants into socks to stave off ticks is just plain ridiculous. All you do when you load up on clothes in the summer - besides sweat - is give your tiny enemy a lifetime's worth of hiding places. Are you more likely to detect a tick crawling on your bare leg or sneaking up your shirt sleeve? So you don't need to dress like a beekeeper outdoors to detect ticks - just check your skin and your dog regularly as you walk. When a tick hitches a ride on you or your dog it doesn't settle in for a meal immediately. It checks out the new digs by wandering around for awhile, typically 4 - 6 hours. Catching a tick at this time is the easiest way to combat it.

TALL TICK TALE #3 - *The Best Way To Avoid Ticks In The First Place Is To Stay Away From Trees*

What is it with irrational fears we harbor about our hair? Bats don't fly into our hair and ticks don't lurk on tree limbs eyeing the tops of our heads like tycoons checking out oceanfront property. Leave your tick-fighting hat at home. Ticks spend most of their time clinging to wispy blades of long grass waiting for a warm-blooded passerby to hitch a ride. The best place way to avoid ticks is to keep your dog and yourself out in the middle of a trail as much as possible.

TALL TICK TALE #4 - *It Is Cold Outside; I Don't Need To Worry About Ticks*

When the summer sun fades away don't stop thinking about ticks - they remain active any time the temperature is above 30 degrees. In the winter, in fact, you may find more ticks on your dog than any other time of the year.

If you want to be outdoors, you aren't going to avoid all ticks. But if you deal with them realistically, you don't need to avoid the outdoors, either. By checking your dog - and yourself - thoroughly after each walk, you can help avoid Lyme disease. Ticks tend to congregate on your dog's ears, between the toes and around the neck and head. Also pay special attention across the center of her back.

"The greatest pleasure of a dog is that you may make a fool of yourself with him, and not only will he not scold you, but will make a fool of himself too."
- Samuel Butler

Outfitting Your Dog For A Hike

These are the basics for taking your dog on a hike:

▸ **Collar.**
  A properly fitting collar should not be so loose as to come off but you should be able to slide your flat hand under the collar.

▸ **Identification Tags.**
  Get one with your veterinarian's phone number as well.

▸ **Bandanna.**
  Can help distinguish him from game in hunting season.

▸ **Leash.**
  Leather lasts forever but if there's water in your dog's future, consider quick-drying nylon.

▸ **Water.**
  Carry 8 ounces for every hour of hiking.

🐾 *I want my dog to help carry water, snacks and other supplies on the trail. Where do I start?*

To select an appropriate dog pack measure your dog's girth around the rib cage. A dog pack should fit securely without hindering the dog's ability to walk normally.

🐾 *Will my dog wear a pack?*

Wearing a dog pack is no more obtrusive than wearing a collar, although some dogs will take to a pack easier than others. Introduce the pack by draping a towel over your dog's back in the house and then having your dog wear an empty pack on short walks. Progressively add some crumpled newspaper and then bits of clothing. Fill the pack with treats and reward your dog from the stash. Soon your dog will associate the dog pack with an outdoor adventure and will eagerly look forward to wearing it.

How much weight can I put into a dog pack?

Many dog packs are sold by weight recommendations. A healthy, well-conditioned dog can comfortably carry 25% to 33% of its body weight. Breeds prone to back problems or hip dysplasia should not wear dog packs. Consult your veterinarian before stuffing the pouches with gear.

How does a dog wear a pack?

The pack, typically with cargo pouches on either side, should ride as close to the shoulders as possible without limiting movement. The straps that hold the dog pack in place should be situated where they will not cause chafing.

What are good things to put in a dog pack?

Low density items such as food and poop bags are good choices. Ice cold bottles of water can cool your dog down on hot days. Don't put anything in a dog pack that can break. Dogs will bang the pack on rocks and trees as they wiggle through tight spots in the trail. Dogs also like to lie down in creeks and other wet spots so seal items in plastic bags. A good use for dog packs when on day hikes around Long Island is trail maintenance - your dog can pack out trash left by inconsiderate visitors before you.

"My dog can bark like a Congressman, fetch like an aide, beg like a press secretary and play dead like a receptionist."
-Gerald Solomon

❖ Are dog booties a good idea?

Although not typically necessary, dog booties can be an asset, especially for the occasional canine hiker whose paw pads have not become toughened. Most Long Island trails are soft under paw but in some places there may be broken glass or roots. Hiking boots for dogs are designed to prevent pads from cracking while trotting across rough surfaces.

❖ What should a doggie first aid kit include?

Even when taking short hikes it is a good idea to have some basics available for emergencies:

- ▸ 4" square gauze pads
- ▸ cling type bandaging tapes
- ▸ topical wound disinfectant cream
- ▸ tweezers
- ▸ insect repellent - no reason to leave your dog unprotected against mosquitoes and biting flies
- ▸ veterinarian's phone number

"I can't think of anything that brings me closer to tears than when my old dog - completely exhausted after a hard day in the field - limps away from her nice spot in front of the fire and comes over to where I'm sitting and puts her head in my lap, a paw over my knee, and closes her eyes, and goes back to sleep. I don't know what I've done to deserve that kind of friend."
-Gene Hill

Low Impact Hiking
With Your Dog

Every time you hike with your dog on the trail you are an ambassador for all dog owners. Some people you meet won't believe in your right to take a dog on the trail. Be friendly to all and make the best impression you can by practicing low impact hiking with your dog:

- Pack out everything you pack in.

- Do not leave dog scat on the trail; if you haven't brought plastic bags for poop removal bury it away from the trail and topical water sources.

- Hike only where dogs are allowed.

- Stay on the trail.

- Do not allow your dog to chase wildlife.

- Step off the trail and wait with your dog while horses and other hikers pass.

- Do not allow your dog to bark - people are enjoying the trail for serenity.

- *Have as much fun on your hike as your dog does.*

Suffolk County Green Key

With the Suffolk County Parks Green Key card residents pay reduced fees for parking and special events. Green key holders also have access to the automated campground reservation system.

Suffolk County residents can obtain a green key by providing:

a) a driver's license,

b) a current Suffolk County property tax receipt or deed,

c) a Suffolk County Voter Registration Card, or

d) an official residential lease for a minimum of nine months.

Green keys are valid for three years from the date of purchase. Discounts apply volunteer firefighters and ambulence personnel. Active military and disabled veterans pay no fees for Suffolk County parks.

Tourist green keys are available for non-residents. These cards are valid for one year from the date of purchase. For more information, call (631) 854-4949 or visit the website at **www.suffolkcountyny. gov.**

"The best thing about a man is his dog."
-French Proverb

New York State Department of Environmental Conservation Permits

A seasonal access permit is required for all activities on all New York State Department of Environmental Conseration (NYSDEC) managed lands on Long Island. The permit is free and valid for three years. For dog owners this requirement most directly affects users of Rocky Point Natural Resources Management Area.

Permits are also required for a variety of special uses. Permits can be obtained in person at:

Sporting License Office, NYSDEC - SUNY

50 Circle Road

Stony Brook, NY 11790

For more information, contact the NYSDEC regional office at (631) 444-0273 or visit the website at **www.dec.ny.gov/outdoor/7780.html**.

"No one appreciates the very special genius of your conversation as a dog does."
-Christopher Morley

Doggin Long Island –
The Best of the Best

BEST ONE-HOUR WORKOUT FOR YOUR DOG:
Laurel Valley County Park (Noyack). A sporty loop takes your dog in and out of kettle depressions and across ridges for almost three miles.

BEST PLACE FOR YOUR DOG (any dog) TO SWIM:
Wades Beach (Shelter Island). The sandy shore on the south side of the island is almost lake-like and the sandy bottom continues out far into the water.

BEST PLACE FOR YOUR DOG (athletic dog) TO SWIM:
Napeague State Park (Promised Land). The waves come fast and furious on the Hampton beaches and this one is no exception.

PRETTIEST HIKE FOR YOUR DOG:
Prosser Pines County Park (Middle Island). The only attraction here is Long Island's oldest grove of white pines but that is enough to enthrall your dog during his adventure here.

BEST HIKE TO VIEWS WITH YOUR DOG:

Shadmoor State Park (Montauk). You won't see anything but the sky above on this hike through dense beach heather but in short time your dog will be hiking on open bluffs above the Atlantic Ocean.

BEST BEACH TO HIKE WITH YOUR DOG:

Fire Island National Seashore (Shirley). The Otis Pike Wilderness Area opens to your dog after Labor Day for seven miles of hiking on the wide, sand beach and behind the dunes.

BEST HALF-HOUR HIKE WITH YOUR DOG:

Walking Dunes, Hither Hills State Park (East Hampton). This 3/4-mile loop travels over and around 80-foot high sand dunes, moving past ghost forests buried in the shifting sands.

MOST HISTORIC HIKE
WITH YOUR DOG:

Camp Hero State Park (Montauk). From the Revolutionary War, when it was used as an artillery practice range, through the Cold War Camp Hero has hosted the United States military.

BEST PLACE TO
CIRCLE A LAKE WITH
YOUR DOG:

Belmont State Park (Babylon). The immortal racehorse Man O' War may have loped on the easy route around the park's center-piece lake.

BEST PLACE TO
LOSE YOURSELF IN
THE WOODS WITH
YOUR DOG:

Edgewood Oak Brush Plains Preserve (Deer Park). No need to limit yourself to a pre-determined route on a hike with your dog around the grounds of a former hospital.

BEST PLACE TO HIKE AND SEE OTHER DOGS:

Gardiner County Park (West Bay Shore). There is no reason to come to this park with a maze of short trails on the Great south Bay without a dog. Not many do.

No Dogs

These are some of the many Long Island parks that do not allow dogs so you don't waste your time:

New York State Parks
Bayard Cutting Arboretum - Oakdale
Bethpage State Park - Farmingdale
Caleb Smith State Park Preserve - Smithtown
Captree State Park - Babylon
Caumsett State Historic Park - Huntington
Cold Spring Harbor State Park - Cold Spring Harbor
Connetquot River State Park - Oakdale
Gilgo State Park - Babylon
Jones Beach State Park - Wantaugh
Nissequoque River State Park - Kings Park
Orient Beach State Park - Orient
Robert Moses State Park - Babylon
Trail View State Park - Huntington
Valley Stream State Park - Valley Stream
Wildwood State Park - Wading River

Nassau County Parks
Dogs are not allowed in ANY county park
but the following do have dog runs:

Bay Park - First Avenue, East Rockaway
Christopher Morley Park - Searington Road, Rosyln-North Hills
Cedar Creek Park - Merrick Road, Seaford
Nickerson Beach Park - Lido Boulevard, Lido
Wantagh Park - Kings Road & Canal Place, Wantagh

Wildlife Refuges
Morton National Wildlife Refuge - Noyack
Target Rock National Wildlife Refuge - Lloyd Neck
Quogue Wildlife Refuge - Quogue
Wertheim National Wildlife Refuge - Shirley

Nature Conservancy Preserves
Accabonic Harbor - East Hampton
Big Woods Preserve - Southampton
Mashomack Preserve - Shelter Island
Montauk Mountain - Montauk
Uplands Farm Sanctuary - Cold Spring Harbor

Nature Centers and Preserves
Massapequa Preserve - Massapequa Park
Muttonwood Preserve - East Norwich
Sands Point Preserve - Sands Point
South Shore Nature Center - East Islip
Sweetbriar Nature Center - Smithtown

O.K. It could have been worse. Let's forget about these and move on to some of the great places where we CAN take our dogs on Long Island trails...

The 30 Best Places To Hike With Your Dog In Long Island...

1
Hither Hills State Park

The Park

In 1879, ten years before his death, Arthur W. Benson, of Brooklyn Gas & Light and Bensonhurst fame, purchased 10,000 acres of government land around Montauk for a little more than $15 an acre. He envisioned his new holdings as a playground for the rich.

A generation later Robert Moses, the visionary New York land planner, saw a different future for Montauk. He wanted a necklace of public parks along the Montauk shores and in 1924 announced plans to condemn 1700 Benson estate acres for the fledgling New York State Parks system.

It took a three-year court battle that wound its way to the New York Supreme Court but Moses prevailed. The enduring jewel of his struggle is Hither Hills State Park that stretches from ocean to bay and is the largest state park in Montauk.

Suffolk County

Phone Number
- (631) 668-2554

Website
- http://nysparks.state.ny.us/ parks/info.asp?parkID=48

Admission Fee
- In season mid-April to mid-November, but only south of Route 27 where dogs are not allowed

Park Hours
- Sunrise to sunset

Directions
- *East Hampton*; parking is available on the north side of Montauk Point State Parkway (Route 27) at the Hither Hills Overlook, one mile east of the split with Old Montauk Highway.

The Walks

For most visitors, Hither Hills is a mile of pristine, dune-backed Atlantic Ocean beach and top-rated campground. With such delights, the 1755-acre park's interior that stretches to Napeague Bay is often overlooked. All the better for canine hikers, who are not welcome on the beach anyway. Miles of informal sandy trails and jeep roads pick through the pitch pine, scrub oak and beach heather.

Of the marked trails, the long-distance *Paumanok Path* that crosses to Montauk is the most prominent. It can be combined with the *Serpent's Back*

Hither Hills is home to the unique walking dunes - 80-foot high piles of sand that are blown more than three feet each year by the strong westerly winds. As the sands shift they completely bury trees and vegetation, eventually moving on and leaving phantom forests of dead trees. A 3/4-mile trail loops through the dunes and giant bowls for you and your dog to poke around the bogs and coastal shrubs up close. Further explorations can take place along the shore of Napeague Harbor and around Goff Point. Parking for the Walking Dunes is at the end of Napeague Harbor Road and is limited to a few cars.

Trail and others to form sporty hiking loops that will delight your dog for hours. Expect plenty of ups and downs as you twist through the pine barrens. Highlights include the bass-stuffed Fresh Pond, panoramic overlooks and the sandy/cobbly shore of Napeague Bay.

Trail Sense: Trail maps are available at the parking lot or park office; the named trails are blazed.

Only the tops of trees buried by sand remain on The Walking Dunes Trail.

Dog Friendliness

Dogs are not permitted anywhere south of Route 27 including the beach and campground but can hike east of Napeague Harbor and south of Napeague Bay.

Traffic

Parking is limited and you may go hours without seeing another trail user. Hunting is allowed during the winter months. Be aware that the tracks of the Long Island Railroad you cross on the trail are active.

Canine Swimming

The swimming is easy for your dog on the sandy beach of Napeague Harbor from the *Walking Dunes Trail* and on the shores of Napeague Bay.

Trail Time

A full day is possible.

2
Montauk Point State Park

The Park

At the eastern tip of Long Island the land rises slightly. The Montaukett tribe who reigned over this area called the hill "Womponamon," an Algonquian word meaning "to the east." Great tribal councils were convened from the point.

During the American Revolution the British Royal Navy controlled Montauk Point, lighting enormous fires on the bluff to guide its warships stationed in nearby Gardiner's Bay. When the British departed after the war the American government quickly realized the importance of a lighthouse on Montauk Point. In 1792 Congress appropriated $255.12 to buy land upon which a light was to be built to guide boats past the perilous rocks. The first whale oil was lit in 1797 in New York's first lighthouse and America's fourth.

Suffolk

Phone Number
- (631) 668-3781

Website
- http://nysparks.state.ny.us/parks/info.asp?parkID=136

Admission Fee
- Yes, on weekends and holidays

Park Hours
- Sunrise to sunset

Directions
- *Montauk*; at the very end of the Sunrise Highway (Route 27).

The Walks

In Montauk Point State Park dogs can only go west of the concession stand which works out well since that is where the trails are. You didn't really want to use the playground did you? There are two trailheads here. The red-blazed trail dives towards the shoreline down a service road and the green-blazed *Money Pond Trail* starts a little ways up the road.

The Money Pond is where the pirate Captain Kidd supposedly stashed two treasure chests but no loot has ever been found. Your dog may feel as if he's discovered gold on this tight, twisty route however. The sandy surface is a delight on the paw and the many dips and rolls are certain to pique any dog's interest.

The *Money Pond Trail* joins the yellow-blazed *Seal Haulout Trail* for a longer journey out to Oyster Pond and the red-blazed stem that closes the loop to the parking lot. Both lead to the shore with occasional side trips to the beach. The further your dog hikes from the point the sandier the beaches become.

Trail Sense: There is a mapboard at the concession stand and the paths are well-marked.

Dog Friendliness
Dogs are allowed west of the parking lot/food stand.

Traffic
There is not a heavy parade of trail users this far out on the island.

Canine Swimming
Fantastic swimming awaits your dog in the usually placid Block Island Sound surf on the northern side of the point.

Trail Time
More than one hour.

The historic Montauk Lighthouse was the first building seen by millions of immigrants sailing to America.

3
Fire Island National Seashore

The Park

The origins of the name Fire Island are lost to obscurity. Perhaps it was a mangled spelling of the Dutch numeral "vier" (4) to identify the number of inlet islands in the area. When Fire Island Beach appeared on charts in the 1850s many believed it referred to land-based pirates who built fires on the open sand to lure cargo ships to their doom on the beach. Some favor the explanation that abundant poision ivy - it turns bright red in the fall - gave the island its colorful moniker.

By any name Fire Island has attracted settlers for centuries, drawn by its bountiful stores of seafood and waterfowl. But by 1964 Fire Island was the only developed barrier island in the United States without any roads and the national seashore was established to keep it that way.

Suffolk

Phone Number
- (631) 289-4810

Website
- www.nps.gov/fiis/index.htm

Admission Fee
- None

Park Hours
- Sunrise to sunset

Directions (Otis Pike Wilderness Area)
- *Shirley*; from the Long Island Expressway take Exit 68 and follow the William Floyd Parkway (Route 46) south to its end.

The Walks

Your dog's adventure at Fire Island is dependent on the time of year. Dogs are not allowed on the beach during piping plover nesting season from March 15 to Labor Day but dogs can still visit Watch Hill and Sailors Haven, each accessible only by passenger ferry. Dogs are allowed on the ferries for a fee. At Watch Hill your dog can trot through the Sunken Forest, where 200-year old holly and hardwood trees bravely battle relentless salt sprays.

The prime time for dogs, however, is after Labor Day in the Otis Pike High Dune Wilderness Area, established by Congress in 1980 to protect 1,400 acres on a seven-mile stretch of oceanfront. Starting at the Wilderness Visitor Center at the eastern end, this spectacular sliver of Fire Island reaches to Watch Hill to the west. The ferries run for a few more weeks after Labor Day so it is possible to execute this hike as a car shuttle, otherwise you will need to hike back from your turn-around point.

Every pawfall for your dog will be on thick, soft sand with little shade so the entire 14-mile round trip is unrealistic. Closely monitor your dog's effort to determine

The **Burma Road** *through the Otis Pike Wilderness Area is not always this well-defined.*

when to head back. A good destination is Old Inlet with an attractive dock off Pelican Island about two miles away. You can do the entire hike on the beach at water's edge or make a loop behind the dunes on the *Burma Road*, a sand path that can be indiscernible and virtually impassable in places.

Trail Sense: A park map is available, useful for orientation and locating landmarks but not necessary for navigation.

Dog Friendliness

Dogs are never allowed on a lifeguarded beach or in Robert Moses State Park; dogs can stay in the Watch Hill campground.

Traffic

Driving is allowed on the beach in the wilderness area.

Canine Swimming

Every day more than 10,000 waves pound the wide sand beach - more than a few will have your dog's name on them. There is also access to the Great South Bay for gentler dog paddling.

Trail Time

Up to a full day.

4
Laurel Valley
County Park

The Park

This hunk of oak-hickory climax forest in an otherwise residential area was purchased by Suffolk County in 1990 less for its beauty than for its deep freshwater deposits. We can't see the valuable pockets of water underground but we sure can appreciate the beauty of this undeveloped 148-acre park.

The Walks

The *Paumanok Path* passes through the park but for canine day hikers the star in Laurel Valley is the 2.5-mile loop trail that shares part of it route with its long-distance cousin. This is a sporty outing for your dog dipping in and out of many kettles and ravines through an interesting woodland landscape.

Suffolk

Phone Number
- None

Website
- None

Admission Fee
- None

Park Hours
- Sunrise to sunset

Directions
- *Noyack*; on Deerfield Road, one mile south of Noyac Road (Route 38). From the Montauk Highway (Route 27) turn north on Deerfield Road in Water Mill. Park along the east side of the road.

Monstrous chunks of glacial ice have left kettle depressions across the park and their meltwater cut numerous ravines. The steep sides of the ravines in turn are ideal for the growing of mountain laurel in the understory and, hence, Laurel Valley. None of the climbs is likely to set your dog to panting but you will reach an overlook of the Noyac Golf and Country Club and perhaps Peconic Bay beyond.

The park serves up a series of curiousities to mark your journey around the loop. A grove of smooth, grey-barked beech trees stand out as they

have blotted out the competition below and a single pitch pine has muscled its way through the canopy.

Scores of black locust trees have proven no match for the stiff Long Island breezes in the park.

But the most striking discovery is a graveyard of black locust trees that have fallen in the forest. This native of the southeast is actually an invasive species. It is one of the hardest and heaviest hardwoods in North America and many dozen have been uprooted in the Laurel Valley forest.

Trail Sense: A trail map is posted at the trailhead kiosk and signs keep the loop trail route separate from the *Paumanok Path*.

Dog Friendliness
Dogs are permitted to hike in Laurel Valley.

Traffic
Foot traffic only and the limited parking will not support much of it.

Canine Swimming
None.

Trail Time
Between one and two hours.

5
David Sarnoff
Pine Barrens Preserve

The Park

Russian immigrant David Sarnoff learned to operate a telegraph key as a boy and went to work for the American Marconi Wireless Telegraph Company, meeting the inventor of the telegraph. Before he was to end his career with the Marconi company and its successor, the Radio Corporation of America (RCA) sixty years later Marconi would oversee the invention of radio, champion the development of television, coordinate the communications for D-Day during World War II and log three decades as President of RCA.

On April 12, 1914 a 20-year Sarnoff went to work as a wireless operator when the technology was still a novelty. That night he picked up faint signals from the icy North Atlantic of the sinking of the *Titanic*. He stayed at his post for 72 straight hours bringing news of the disaster to the world. After that all ships were required to have wireless. In the 1920s Sarnoff directed the development of this property as the receiving hub for RCA's revolutionary transatlantic wireless radio communication network.

Suffolk

Phone Number
- (631) 444-0273

Website
- www.dec.ny.gov/
animals/27036.html

Admission Fee
- None

Park Hours
- Sunrise to sunset

Directions
- *Riverhead*; on Route 104, about two miles south of Riverhead traffic cirle. Parking is available in a lot on the west side of the highway.

The Walks

At one time pitch pine and scrub oak barrens covered 25% of all Long Island but today fewer than 100,000 acres remain and these 2,000+ acres are among the largest contiguous swaths of pine barrens remaining. Two canine hiking loops have been carved in the preserve, each reached by a lengthy connector trail, blazed in yellow.

The *Blue Loop* is the shorter of the two circles, about 2.5 miles. Since the acidic soil delays the decay of leaves and organic matter, prescribed burns are necessary to clear the burgeoning tinder box. These burns are evident on the *Blue Loop*. This route crosses high-speed traffic on Route 104 so that makes the longer *Red Loop* more attractive to dog owners.

You will see this scene for hours on the trails in the David Sarnoff Pine Barrens Preserve.

It requires a lengthy 1.25-mile lead-in to reach the *Red Loop* but your dog won't complain while trotting the soft sandy trail. You and your dog will need to go single-file on much of this hike that has been routed past kettle depressions and picturesque stands of pines. In some places the huckleberry and blueberry constrain the path so as to brush each leg. This is easy going for your dog, however, with no real climbs, just dips and rolls through the pine barrens.

Trail Sense: There is a mapboard but nothing to take along; the paths are energetically blazed but expect a missing marker tree along the way.

Dog Friendliness
Dogs are allowed to hike these trails.
Traffic
Foot traffic only and you will be alone most of the way.
Canine Swimming
These pine barrens filter an underground aquifer of between three and five trillion gallons and occasionally a woodland pond has formed to refresh your dog.
Trail Time
At least one hour to finish the *Blue Loop* and two for the *Red*.

6
Hubbard County Park

The Park

John Jacob Astor owned this land on the south shore of Flanders Bay when he was the richest man in America in the early 1800s. Much of the ancestral forest was logged at that time and the tidal Mill Creek was dammed to power a saw mill. Through most of the 1800s the Hubbard family homesteaded here, clearing more land, farming and raising chickens.

In 1937, financier Edward Francis (E.F.) Hutton purchased the Hubbard land to use as a private hunting preserve. He renovated the family home to create the Black Duck Lodge. By the 1970s escalating taxes and residential development forced the closure of many of Long Island's gun clubs. The Black Duck Lodge and the neighboring Flanders Gun Club were acquired by Suffolk County and designated an undeveloped county park.

Suffolk

Phone Number
- None

Website
- None

Admission Fee
- None

Park Hours
- Sunrise to sunset

Directions
- *Hampton Bays*; from the Sunrise Highway (Route 27), take Exit 65 North on Route 24. After two miles turn right on Red Creek Road. A gated entrance is on the left and there is room to park on the shoulder of the road.

The Walks

Most of the extended canine hiking at Hubbard County Park involves crossing active roads but there are a series of road/trails that branch around the property, leading to a variety of adventures for your dog. The *Red Owl Trail* hikes to the shore of Flanders Bay and a "ghost forest" of Atlantic cedar stumps visible at low tide. The stumps are silent testament to the rising sea levels along Long Island's north shore. This trail is closed to the public between April 15 and August 15 for osprey nesting.

Bonus

After emerging from winter hibernation turtles can be seen on the roads and trails at Hubbard County Park. Five types of the reptile inhabit the park: Box Turtles (brown to olive and yellowish); Spotted Turtles (smooth black with yellow spots); Mud Turtles (smooth olive to dark brown); Diamond-backed Terrapins (polygonal with concentric circles); and Snapping Turtles (ridged shell with a saw-toothed tail). Snappers are Long Island's largest common turtles and can inhabit any permanent body of freshwater. Although placid in the water, where they often remain buried in the mud with just their eyes showing, the turtles should not be approached on land as they can deliver a painful bite if jostled.

A short loop around the historic Black Duck Lodge visits marshes and forests and the old Flanders gun Club can be reached to the west of Mill Creek. Along the trails your dog can still sniff the remains of old duck blinds. This is all easy going for your dog on soft surface trails that can get muddy in the low-lying tidal grounds.

The marquee trail in the park is the *Black Owl Loop* that connects to Sears Bellows Park and requires two hazardous crossings of Route 24 to complete its five miles. Across Red Creek Road to the east *Pine Barrens Trail* checks out the freshwater Penny Pond.

Trail Sense: Pick up a trailmap at the entrance to Sears Bellows park across Route 24; the main trails are marked with plastic diamonds but don't be surprised if many are missing.

Dog Friendliness

Dogs are allowed to trot where so many of their ancestors once worked the marshes.

Traffic

Hubbard County Park is lightly visited with most people migrating to its more developed twin, Sears Bellow County Park.

Canine Swimming

There is access for your water-loving dog to the the tidal Hubbard Creek at a canoe launch, Penny Pond and Cow Yard Beach on Flanders Bay.

Trail Time

Several hours possible.

7
Gardiner County Park

The Park

In 1635 military engineer Lion Gardiner sailed to America to build a fort at the mouth of the Connecticut River during the Pequot War. After the war, rather than returning to England, he crossed Long Island Sound to look for a new home. For the price of some cloth, a gun, some powder and "a large black dog" Gardiner purchased a 3,000-acre island from the Montaukett Indians and Sachem Wyandanch.

In 1653 a raiding party of Niantic Indians attacked the Montaukett village on Montauk Point, killing more than 30 and taking prisoner the daughter of Wyandanch. To help his friend, Gardiner sailed to Rhode Island and paid a handsome ransom to bring her home. This led to Gardiner's acquiring an additional 100,000 acres, becoming the largest landowner in Long Island history. Part of his property included this parkland on the Great South Bay that was acquired by Suffolk County in 1971.

Suffolk

Phone Number
- (631) 854-0935

Website
- www.co.suffolk.ny.us/webt-emp1.cfm?dept=10&id=880

Admission Fee
- None

Park Hours
- Sunrise to sunset

Directions
- *West Bay Shore*; on the Montauk Highway (Route 27), east of the Robert Moses Causeway.

The Walks

Come to Gardiner's Park on a beautiful weekend day and you will likely see a full parking lot - and each of those 100 cars has brought at least one dog. If your dog just wants a short walk there is a *Canine Loop* through an open field to the west of the parking lot. For a dog looking for a game of fetch, he can find it in the field behind the main lot.

Trail dogs will head down *Beach Road* that runs down to Great South Bay. Once there, your dog can play on a crescent sand beach to the right. To the left the shore is muddier but still offers swimming opportunities. Crossing back through the marsh on *Beach Road* you can use *Plover Road* to complete a hiking loop of Gardiner Park. These sandy-based trails are all paw-friendly, even squishy in wet times. A maze of short connecting trails can be sampled to create alternate routes on return visits or a second tour of the park.

Trail Sense: A park map is posted on an information board but you can't get lost on the unmarked trails in this 231-acre dog paradise.

Dog Friendliness
This is the dog-friendliest park on Long Island and poop bags are available at the trailhead.

Traffic
For a communal dog walk, come to Gardiner Park.

Canine Swimming
The gentle waves of Great South Bay will beckon even the most timid dog to try a swim.

Trail Time
About one hour.

The shoreline of Great South Bay is open to your dog at Gardiner County Park.

8
Edgewood Oak Brush Plains Preserve

The Park

In 1927 the State of New York built the largest psychiatric hospital the world had ever seen on 825 acres among the farms of Long Island. At its peak, Pilgrim State Hospital housed 13,875 patients. In the early 1940s the U.S. Army established another hospital next door for tuberculosis care and treatment of shell-shocked war veterans.

When World War II ended, the Army turned the facility over to the state which operated it as the Edgewood State Hospital for the next quarter-century. Edgewood closed in 1971 and suffered through a two-decade period of vandalism and neglect. Finally in 1989 the hospital complex and tallest building in western Suffolk County (229 feet high) was demolished.

The property was saved from development by State Senator Owen Johnson and today is part of the Long Island's 1,400 remaining acres of ecologically unique oak brush plains, which once covered 60,000 acres extending eastward from the Hempstead plains.

Suffolk
Phone Number - None
Website - www.dec.ny.gov/out-door/7815.html
Admission Fee - None
Park Hours - Sunrise to sunset
Directions - *Deer Park*; take Exit 53 south from the Long Island Expressway on Commack Road. A generous parking area is on the left side of the road.

The Walks

The main hiking route through the Edgewood site is a blue-blazed route that tickles the edges of the 843-acre preserve. The full circuit covers over three miles but can be shortened on the Old Commack Road (a closed coarse sand thoroughfare) or any of a number

Trotting through the oak brush plains.

of other unmarked old roads. The entire preserve is virtually flat and, despite what its name implies, offers plenty of shade on a hot day. Under paw your dog will find a mix of pebbly sand and broken asphalt. This is a great place to get lost with your dog for a couple of hours.

Trail Sense: No maps but you won't bemoan the lack of prescribed hiking routes.

Dog Friendliness
Dogs are allowed to hike these trails.
Traffic
No motorized vehicles and the terrain isn't challenging enough to attract many mountain bikers or many hikers for that matter.
Canine Swimming
Not here.
Trail Time
Several hours possible.

9
Shadmoor
State Park

The Park

This land was purchased by the first European settlers from the Montaukett Indians late in the 1600s. The open plains on bluffs above the Atlantic Ocean were used used for grazing cattle and Shadmoor was still open grassland when the United States government established Camp Wikoff as a quarantine for soldiers returning from the Spanish-American War in 1898.

After the war in Cuba the servicemen were riddled with tropical fevers. Over 20,000 soldiers recuperated here; 257 died. Among those who spent time in Camp Wikoff was Colonel Theodore Roosevelt and his regiment of Rough Riders.

Suffolk

Phone Number
- None

Website
- http://nysparks.state.ny.us/parks/info.asp?parkID=83

Admission Fee
- None

Park Hours
- Sunrise to sunset

Directions
- *Montauk*; on the south side of Route 27, one-half mile east of the village.

Shadmoor once again became important to the military during World War II when the Army used it for artillery practice and coastal defense. Two large concrete bunkers were built - the first permanent structures on the property as Camp Wikoff had been a canvas tent base. The bunkers are still standing in the park that was acquired in 2000.

The Walks

The hiking goal at Shadmoor is the half-mile of oceanfront bluffs that overlook the Atlantic. There are two ways to get to accomplish this. The most direct route is a gentle uphill climb on abandoned Shad Lane. If you don't make a quick detour to examine the World War II bunker this journey with your dog over the wide, wood-chip path will take less than 20 minutes.

The round-about way is on the red-blazed *Roosevelt Run Trail* that loops around the perimeter of the 99-acre park. The once open plains have given way to a dense cover of maritime heath producing a tunnel effect for much of the journey. Once on the bluffs the hike opens up behind a low rail fence with views as far into the Atlantic Ocean as your dog can see.

Continue downhill on th esomewhat eroded footpath to the east and the trail leaves the state park and meanders into Rheinstein Park, operated by the town. Here your dog can trot down to the Ditch Plains Beach below the bluffs for play in the ocean. Retrace your steps back to Shadmoor or try one of the unmarked trails through the beach heath maze.

Hiking the ocean bluffs at Shadmoor State Park will inspire any dog.

Trail Sense: A park map is available at the trailhead kiosk.

Dog Friendliness
Dogs are allowed throughout the park.
Traffic
Bikes are allowed but this is mostly a foot traffic park.
Canine Swimming
Down on the beach is all the swimming your water-loving dog can take.
Trail Time
More than one hour, depending on how long you stay on the beach.

10
Long Pond Greenbelt

The Park

Water is the dominant theme of the Long Pond Greenbelt, stretching from its creation by glacial activity over 20,000 years ago to its well-lubricated present. Some 30 bodies of water including saltwater ponds, freshwater ponds and tidal ponds are included in the 1,100 acres bounded by the Sag Harbor Turnpike and Sagg Road.

In the 1800s a mile-long trench was dug among several ponds to juice the water flow for a mill to operate on Otter Pond. Later a dam was built at the north end of Long Pond to provide public water for Sag Harbor.

This aquatic diversity has created a wonderland for botanists - there are more rare plant species here than anywhere in New York. More than three dozen are globally threatened.

The preserve began in 1969 and over the years parcels of land have collected from the town, county and state to builf the Greenbelt from Ligonee Creek in Sag Harbor to Sagaponack Pond in Sagaponack.

Suffolk

Phone Number
- None

Website
- longpondgreenbelt.org/

Admission Fee
- None

Park Hours
- Sunrise to sunset

Directions
- *Sag Harbor*; from Bridgehampton on Route 27 take the Bridgehampton-Sag Harbor Turnpike north to Mahashimuet Park on the right. Park in front of the playground but be certain not to enter the park - there are more NO DOGS signs per square inch here than any place on Long Island. The trailhead is evident at an opening in the woods to your right, past an information board.

The Walks

The backbone of the Long Pond Greenbelt is the *Old Railway Spur* that hauled passengers and freight between Bridgehampton Train Station and Long Wharf in Sag Harbor between 1870 and 1939. One of the most prized cargoes was ice from Round Pond destined to New York City. The railway was pulled

up for steel in World War II and the predictably flat route now makes an ideal trotting surface for dogs.

There are more than nine miles of trails here, including little detours to the old water works and the dam. For a long, leisurely loop point your dog south on the *Old Railway Spur*, turn left on the *Crooked Pond Path* and head back on the *Sprig Tree Path*. For shorter outings, there are many combinations open. Under paw your dog will find a sandy, pebbly mix often obscured by oak leaves.

Trail Sense: Most of the trails are unmarked but you can study a map on the information board before setting out. Even without a map you can wander with confidence knowing the park never extends too far east or west.

Dog Friendliness
Dogs are welcome to hike these pleasant trails.

Traffic
No motor vehicles and the wide main routes afford plenty of passing room.

Canine Swimming
Your water-loving dog will find many spots to delay your hike here. There is a boat ramp at Long Pond off Widow Gavitts Road.

Trail Time
Many hours possible.

11

Theodore Roosevelt County Park

The Park

Deep Hollow Ranch was founded in 1658 and claims to be the birthplace of the American cowboy. There was no need to build fences; the Atlantic Ocean on the south and Block Island Sound to the north provided natural boundaries. For over 250 years cattle, sheep and horses grazed here - as many as 6,000 in peak years. The ranch is still operating today, moving past 350 years, offering trail rides.

As late as the 1700s only three houses stood on the eastern tip of Long Island, spaced three miles apart. From west to east they were First House in Napeague that was to burn, Second House in Montauk and Third House that now houses park headquarters. In 1879 Arthur Bensen bought all the land from Napeague to Montauk Point and lived in Third House. He hoped to create a resort but when his plans failed he sold out to the federal government who built Camp Wikoff during the Spanish-American War and used Third House as its headquarters.

Suffolk
Phone Number - (631) 852-7878
Website - www.co.suffolk.ny.us/webt-emp1.cfm?dept=10&id=888
Admission Fee - None
Park Hours - Sunrise to sunset
Directions - *Montauk*; on the north side of Montauk Highway, east of the Village past East Lake Drive. The nature trails are down East Lake Drive on the right side of the road.

Checking out the wildlife on Big Reed Pond.

The Walks

Theodore Roosevelt County Park maintains an extensive trail system but canine hikers are best served at the *Big Reed Pond Nature Trails*. Here, a triple-stacked loop of colored trails pile up almost three miles of first-rate hiking with your dog. This is one of the few interpretive trails on Long Island.

The routes curve pleasingly with a few short hills thrown into the mix. Your dog will be sheltered the entire way, save for the open setting of a former Montaukett village site. The trail system trips through a succession of plant communties from tidal marshes to wet meadows to upland hickory forests to a recovering sand mine.

The hiking is easy for your dog in Roosevelt Park so you may want to push further east past Big Reed Pond to adjacent natural areas.

Trail Sense: A park map is available in the office and "you-are-here" map-boards are present at the trailhead and key junctions on the well-blazed trails.

Dog Friendliness
Dogs are allowed on the trails and the in the camper-only campground.
Traffic
Bikes and horses can use the park trails, mostly on the sand service roads.
Canine Swimming
Outer Beach behind the campground on Long Island Sound offers excellent dog paddling - you can hike down a service road to the beach. A small beach on Lake Montauk opposite the trailhead serves up superb doggie dips.
Trail Time
More than one hour.

12
Calverton Ponds

The Park

This 350-acre coastal plain pond ecosystem is one of the most unique wetland ecosystems in North America. The ponds are topographical depressions that intersect groundwater and are fed through porous sand, not streams like most ponds. Water levels rise and fall with the rainfall causing an adaptive plant community that can survive in times of plenty and times of scarcity. More than 30 of these plant species are considered rare and threatened - the most in New York.

The Walks

This is one of the loveliest hikes you can take with your dog on Long Island, more like a stroll down a pine-lined country lane. The wide road/trails slip among three tranquil coastal ponds.

The trail system visits all three ponds. You can circle Block Pond on the white-blazed trail, returning on the yellow-blazed path. The yellow-blazed route also visits the back shores of Fox Pond but you will need to retrace your steps here. You need to keep your dog on the trail to protect this fragile environment but that is easy on the wide passageways. This is all easy hiking for your dog on soft, straw-covered paths.

Trail Sense: A plastic-coated map is kept at the trailhead and the routes are well-marked.

Suffolk

Phone Number
- None

Website
- www.nature.org/wherewe-work/northamerica/states/new-york/preserves/art10987.html

Admission Fee
- None

Park Hours
- Sunrise to sunset

Directions
- *Manorville*; from the Long Island Expressway take Exit 70 and turn north. After less than one mile turn right on Ryerson Avenue at the T-intersection. Turn right on North Street after crossing the railroad tracks and bear left on Wading River Manor Road when the road splits. Make your second right onto Old River Road. A small parking area is a half-mile down on the left.

Death and killing are going on all around
you in this tranquil spot. It takes a special plant to
make a life in the nutrient-challenged environment
of the Pine Barrens. Some have evolved to draw
their sustenance from juicy insects.
Along the shores of Calverton Ponds is a good place
to observe these insectivorious plants.
Ewer-shaped pitcher plants lure insects with
the promise of a sweet nectar meal from which
they slip into a deadly trap for consumption by a
cocktail of digestive fluids in the pitcher.
Tiny hairs pointing downward prevent the doomed
victims from crawling to freedom.
Sundews secrete a gooey substance to snare their
next meal. The leaves of water-based bladderworts
have tiny trapdoors that open when nature's
smorgasbord floats by.
In the air during the summer look over the water
for colorful damselflies. These ferocious hunters
are globally threatened with many species found
only on the waters of Long Island.

Dog Friendliness

Dogs are restricted to the trails.

Traffic

No bikes, no motor vehicles and no horses allowed; the limited parking guarantees light visitation.

Canine Swimming

This protected preserve is not the place to satisfy your water-loving dog.

Trail Time

Plan on between one and two hours.

The canine hike along Sandy Pond is one of the most peaceful on Long Island.

13
Rocky Point Natural
Resources Management Area

The Park

After World War I the Radio Corporation of America (RCA) gobbled up 6,000 acres in Rocky Point to develop the world's largest and most powerful wireless transmitting station. The site included a research and development lab and an administration building that connected to a series of land-consuming long-wave radio towers. Construction began in 1920 on the Spanish-style main building meant to evoke a Hollywood mansion. "Radio Central" began operations on Nov. 5, 1921, on a signal from President Warren Gamiel Harding, who formally opened the station by sending a radiogram from Washington addressed to all nations.

By the early 1960s, with the advent of satellites, most of the original long-wave towers that had stood at Radio Central were dismantled and removed. The installation shut down in 1978 and RCA donated Rocky Point and its twin receiving station in Riverhead to the State for $1 each. In 1993, the New York State Legislature enacted the Long Island Pine Barrens Protection Act, providing both the Sarnoff Preserve and Rocky Point the highest level of protection.

Suffolk

Phone Number
- (631) 444-0273

Website
- www.dec.ny.gov/out-door/7780.html

Admission Fee
- None

Park Hours
- Sunrise to sunset

Directions
- *Rocky Point*; the park is dissected by Route 21, Rocky Point Road, south of Route 25A. Parking is available on Rocky Point Road, Route 25A and on the east side of Whiskey Road.

The Walks

Rocky Point is laced with dozens of miles of trails dedicated to hiking, mountain biking and equestrians. If you keep your dog on the hiking-only trails you are essentially signing on for a ten-mile loop around the entire property. Your canine hiking day can be short-circuited, however, by using the multi-use trails to work your way back to the trailhead.

The northern part of Rocky Point sports more hills than the numbingly flat southern sections but this is easy trotting for your dog throughout. Oaks dominate the forest, sharing the stage with pines only grudgingly. Rocky Point is also the eastern terminus of the _Paumanok Path_ that eventually touches the Atlantic Ocean just short of Montauk Point and its white blazes mingle every now and then with the loop trail.

Trail Sense: The trails are well-marked with blazes and distance signs, as is the wont of the state Department of Environmental Conservation. The hiking loop is comprised by the joining of the _Blue Trail_ and _Red Trail_.

Dog Friendliness
Dogs are allowed to hike throughout the management area.

Traffic
The hiking trails are reserved for foot traffic; the sandy roads and fire breaks can host horses and bikes should you venture there.

Canine Swimming
Canine hikers only need apply.

Trail Time
A full half-day to complete the loop around the property.

14

Camp Hero
State Park

The Park

The federal government first established a base at the strategic tip of Long Island in 1929, naming the fort for Major General Andrew Hero, Jr., who was the Army's Chief of Coast Artillery at the time. During World War II in 1942, with German U-boats menacing the East Coast, the installation was bulked up with seaplane hangars, barracks and docks and renamed Camp Hero.

All the buildings were built to look like an innocuous New England fishing village. Concrete bunkers had windows painted on them and base buildings sprouted ornamental roofs with fake dormers. The gymnasium was made to look like a church with a false steeple. At its peak, the camp housed 600 enlisted men and 37 officers.

In 1947 Camp Hero was deactivated but revived in the 1950s as a site for Antiaircraft Artillery training. The military left for good in 1978 and after an effort to turn Montauk Point into a resort destination was thwarted the land was bounced from the U.S. Department of the Interior to the State of New York, finally becoming a state park in 2002.

The Walks

There is plenty of unique wandering to be found for your your dog in old Camp Hero. The *Paumanok Path* begins (or ends) its journey across Long Island here. Part of your dog's hiking day can follow part of the Old Montauk Highway that was the principle artery though the South Fork until the Montauk State Parkway was constructed. You can explore the buildings still standing in the military area. Bunkers and odd structures are seemingly around every turn.

Your dog will find elevation changes as the trails visit the top of fragile bluffs and work down to cobble beaches. Although much of the trails are broken macadam or sandy jeep roads you can also find traditional woods walking on paths like the *Battery 113 Trail*. Oh, and stick to the roads and trails - it is not impossible to stumble upon unexploded ordnance.

Trail Sense: A trail map is available in the park.

Dog Friendliness
Dogs are allowed throughout Camp Hero.
Traffic
This is not a busy place but you can see a bike or a horse.
Canine Swimming
The trails lead down to the Atlantic Ocean where the surf is often frisky enough to dissuade all but the most avid dog paddler.
Trail Time
Several hours possible.

The rough surf at Camp Hero's cobble beach may intimidate some dogs.

15
Prosser Pines Nature Preserve

The Park

In 1812, William "Uncle Billy" Dayton planted a grove of white pine seedlings on the family farm. He obtained the seedlings from the neighboring Edwards farm that were growing from seedlings brought back from Quebec by French-and-Indian War veteran Jonathan Edwards.

The Dayton family nurtured the pine grove through several generations until the farm was sold to George Prosser in 1889. Prosser was an even more attentive steward of the pines, some of which had grown to over 90 feet tall.

Prosser would not allow standing trees to be cut - even when trees toppled in storms were shown to produce over 2000 board feet of lumber. He allowed the public to picnic in his grove and lobbied the township to expand his 30 acres of pines. As development quickened following World War II worried local residents agitated to protect the famous trees. Finally in 1969 Suffolk County purchased the pine plantation, preserving forever the largest white pine forest on Long Island.

Suffolk

Phone Number
- (631) 852-5500

Website
- www.nps.gov/guis

Admission Fee
- None

Park Hours
- Sunrise to sunset

Directions
- *Middle Island*; on Yaphank-Middle Island Road, south of Route 25. From the Long Island Expressway take Exit 66 North (Sills Rd). Bear left at the flashing light (Middle Island/Yaphank Rd). The park entrance is on the right, past Cathedral Pines County Park.

The Cathedral Pines can make a Great Dane appear small.

The Walks

An outing with your dog in the Prosser Pines is like no other on Long Island. The trails here disappear under a thick carpet of pine straw, the sun struggles to reach the ground, and you wander through scented corridors completely bereft of understory.

The park slopes gently uphill and after you ascend the grade the legacy pines thin away, replaced by a younger, airier woodland. The ridge affords splendid views back into the dark cathedral.

Old pine logs have been piled into a spacious tipi in the park.

Trail Sense: There is an occasional signpost but not enough to rely on - not that you will be in any hurry to take your dog away from this magical place.

Dog Friendliness
Dogs are allowed to ramble through the Cathedral Pines.
Traffic
Foot traffic only.
Canine Swimming
None.
Trail Time
About one hour.

16

West Hills County Park

The Park

The Whitmans were a pioneering family in the West Hills and by the time Walter, the second of nine children, was born in Huntington on May 31, 1819 his ancestors had lived here for over one hundred and fifty years. Walt Whitman only lived in the family's cedar shingle house until he was four years old when his father moved the clan to Brooklyn. But America's "greatest poet" never lost his affection for the ancestral grounds and returned often. In 1850 he wrote, "West Hills is a romantic and beautiful spot." In Whitman's day, before the second-growth hardwood forest reclaimed the slopes, he could look to the shores of Connecticut in one direction and watch the packet ships off Fire Island in the other.

Suffolk

Phone Number
- (631) 854-4423

Website
- www.co.suffolk.ny.us/webt-emp1.cfm?dept=10&id=872

Admission Fee
- None

Park Hours
- Sunrise to sunset

Directions
- *Melville*; take Exit 49S off the Long Island Expressway and head north on Route 110. Make the immediate left on Gwynne Road after crossing the Northern State Parkway. Make the first right onto Sweet Hollow Road and the expansive parking lot at the dog run is on the right.

The Walks

The marquee trail in the West Hills is - naturally - the white-blazed *Walt Whitman Trail*. Interlocked with the park's blue-blazed route it forms a satisfying canine loop of about four miles. The highlight is the arrival at High Hill, later named Jayne's Hill for a prominent land-owning family that is marked with a commemorative boulder to Whitman.

The "hills" provide only sporadic challenges for any trail dog. Once you reach the pebbly dirt on the ridges the elevation gains are scarcely noticeable. This entire canine hike is conducted under the shaded canopy of hardwoods with a healthy understory of mountain laurel and dogwood.

For additional trail time with your dog, head off down a panoply of unmarked side paths or cross Sweet Hollow Road for even more canine hiking.

Trail Sense: Once you locate the trailhead (behind the picnic area) you will be fine but there are no maps or signs to direct you there.

Dog Friendliness
Dogs are allowed to hike these trails.

Traffic
Horses are common on weekends and during good weather.

Canine Swimming
Your dog may get a few strokes in Toad Pond, just east of Jayne's Hill.

Trail Time
More than one hour.

17
Sears Bellows County Park

The Park

Once the site of the Flanders Club for sportsmen, the 979-acre county park is named for the two families that once owned much of the land. In 1963 Suffolk County purchased the first of its land to create Sears Bellow park.

The Walks

The tail of your trail dog may droop a bit when bounding from the car in the Sears Bellows parking lot, greeted by an off-limits beach and a walk through a busy campground.

But chin up. Once you clear the bustle of the developed part of the park and start down the blue-blazed footpath your dog's mood will brighten immediately.

Suffolk

Phone Number
- (631) 852-8290

Website
- www.co.suffolk.ny.us/webt-emp1.cfm?dept=10&id=886

Admission Fee
- Yes, in summer

Park Hours
- 8:00 a.m to sunset

Directions
- *Hampton Bays*; follow Sunrise Highway to Exit 65 North. Follow the road (Route 24) to Bellows Pond Road and turn left. The park entrance is on your right.

The dominant natural features of the extensive park trail system are two lovely, pine-shaded ponds, Bellows and Sears, appropriately. The trail - sometimes narrow - between them is draped in large pines that often lean across the wide road/trail to touch boughs. There are long straightaways and some rolling terrain on these easy-going piney hikes. More than a dozen ponds are situated throughout the park. Dirt roads can be used for extended canine hiking here, including passing under the Sunrise Highway.

Trail Sense: A trailmap can be had at the park entrance.

Long Island with its humid climate, abundance of running water and sandy soil is ideal for raising ducks. Some of the largest duck farms in the world have been located on Long Island. In the 1930s there were 90 duck farms around Riverhead alone. In 1931 one of those duck farmers, Martin Maurer, built a retail poultry store in the shape of a 20-foot high Peking duck. Dubbed the "Big Duck" from the beginning, the buidling was constructed on a wood frame with wire mesh, sheathed in concrete and painted white. The eyes were Ford Model "T" tail lights.

In 1937, the 16,500-pound Big Duck was moved from its perch on West Main Street in Riverhead four miles southeast to Flanders, where it became a Long Island landmark before closing in 1984. Suffolk County rescued Big Duck from a wrecking ball and placed it at the entrance of Sears Bellows park in 1988.

Big Duck moved downed the road in 2007 where it now houses a retail gift shop operated by the Friends for Long Island Heritage.

Dog Friendliness
Dogs are welcome on the trails but not on the beach.
Traffic
Bikes can also be found on the trail but you can expect long stretches of time alone with your dog in Sears Bellows County Park.
Canine Swimming
There is plenty of access to freshwater ponds for your dog to practice his best dog paddle.
Trail Time
An hour or more is possible, especially if you continue outside the park.

18
Pine Barrens Trail Information Center

The Park

The Pine Barrens is Long Island's premier ecosystem and one of the Northeast United State's greatest natural treasures. There is a greater diversity of plant and animal species here than anywhere in all of New York.

Prized for the beauty of the pitch pine and oak forests that grace the landscape, the Pine Barrens are also working hard for the citizens of Long Island. The sandy soils overlie the source of the greatest quantity of the purest drinking water on the island and filter virtually every drop into a single system of underground reservoirs, known as aquifers. This led the federal Environmental Protection Agency to designate the aquifer system as the nation's first Sole Source Aquifer, requiring special protection.

Suffolk

Phone Number
- (631) 852-3449

Website
- www.co.suffolk.ny.us/webt-emp1.cfm?dept=10&id=885

Admission Fee
- None

Park Hours
- Sunrise to sunset

Directions
- *Manorville*; take Exit 70 off the Long Island Expressway and go north on Route 111. The Visitor Center is only 1/4 mile away on the right.

The Walks

Your dog has a choice here: a low-key trot or a spirited woodland ramble. The *Wampmissick Trail* is a 3/4-mile, handicap accessible loop that travels along finely ground gravel. Even with a rest on one of the trail benches or a stop to pick wild blueberries, this spin is just an appetizer for your dog.

The *Red/Yellow Trail* breaks away from the interpretive loop down a narrow, leaf-covered single track where the adventure for your dog begins. The rolling route loops back to the departure point (make sure you turn left after re-crossing the road) or takes off across the Long Island Railroad for a long-distance canine hike. There was a Wampmissick train station here as early as 1852.

This is classic woodland hiking for your dog on a serpentine path, shaded all the way. Look for a lone glacial erratic along the *Red Trail*. The hike does suffer from its proximity to the Long Island Expressway - even with the trees as a buffer, the drone of traffic never really disappears.

Trail Sense: Brochures are available and the trails well-marked, although the split of the red trail is not obvious.

Dog Friendliness
Dogs are allowed on the trails.
Traffic
No bikes, no horses, not many hikers.
Canine Swimming
All the water is underground here.
Trail Time
Less than one hour to several hours possible.

The roomy Wampmissick Trail, *with its paw-friend-ly packed clay surface, is so agreeeable you may decide to take your dog around a second time.*

19
Southaven County Park

The Park

This land situated along the Carmans River formed the western boundary of the massive landholdings of William "Tangier" Smith. The former mayor of Tangier, Morocco, Smith landed in America in 1686 and eventually bought 81,000 acres all the way to Riverhead. He oversaw his empire from the Manor of St. George that he built at the mouth of the river a few miles to the south.

At this time the river was known as the Connecticut River and was the center for many small industries. Tar and turpentine from the plentiful pine trees was such a thriving business that by 1705 the town began to tax it. The settlement that grew up around the tarring business and was called "South Haven" shortened from "South Brookhaven."

Mills began to replace the resin buckets and the most prosperous belonged to Samuel Carman. His house was so large it operated as a post office, tavern and store. New Yorkers arriving from the city to hunt ducks commonly said they were going to "Carman's river," and so it became.

Suffolk
Phone Number - (631) 854-1414
Website - www.co.suffolk.ny.us/webt-emp1.cfm?dept=10&id=878
Admission Fee - None
Park Hours - Sunrise to sunset
Directions - *Brookhaven*; just north of the Sunrise Parkway (Route 27), west of the Yaphank Avenue exit (57) and west of the William Floyd Parkway exit (58). The park entrance is on the north side of Victory Road.

The Walks

Southaven is primarily a picnic park with enough facilities to accommodate 1000 people on a summer afternoon. But there is plenty here to entertain an active trail dog as well. Push beyond the picnic groves and pick out a sandy road into the trees. Nothing is marked so come with a mind to enjoy an afternoon of free form hiking with your dog here - don't come with a due back date, just wander.

Work your way north through the open pine forest to create a big canine hiking loop. Sample some side trails. To the east you'll reach the river where your dog can cool off, elsewhere you'll ramble through open grass fields.

Your dog will find the open fields in Southaven County Park a nice change-up from the typical woodland trails on Long Island.

Trail Sense: You will see an arrow on a tree or a stray blaze but no map is handy to explain their meaning.

Dog Friendliness
Dogs are permitted on the park trails and in the campground.

Traffic
Southaven is a busy park in season but almost forgotten when the weather chills. Horse riding is popular but the sandy surfaces keep many bikes away.

Canine Swimming
Excellent dog paddling can be had on the banks of Carmans River.

Trail Time
More than one hour.

20
Belmont Lake State Park

The Park

August Belmont, Jr. inherited the Belmont banking house from his father, from which he helped fund the building of the New York subway. But he is best remembered as a horsemen, serving as the first president of thoroughbred racing's ruling body, the Jockey Club, and creating Belmont Park.

Belmont lived most of his life on his 1,100-acre estate here, nurturing one of America's greatest racing stables. During World War I, Belmont volunteered in France with the U.S. Army at the age of 65, causing him to disband his legendary stable. One of the last foals raised here was named by his wife in honor of his military service: Man o' War.

After August Belmont died in 1924 the family mansion was used as Long Island State Park Commision Administration Headquarters. It was razed in 1935 for a new headquarters.

Suffolk

Phone Number
- (631) 667-5055

Website
- nysparks.state.ny.us/parks/info.asp?parkID=159

Admission Fee
- Yes, in season

Park Hours
- Sunrise to sunset

Directions
- *Babylon*; at Exit 38 of the Southern State Parkway. To reach the southern end of the park, go to Exit 39. Head south on Deer Park Avenue, cross over Sunrise Highway, and one mile further, turn right onto Park Avenue. Turn right into Babylon Village Park.

The Walks

The star walk for your dog in Belmont Lake State Park is a pleasing circumnavigation of the centerpiece lake. At a languid pace this trip on the big, curving loop will take you about an hour to complete with your dog. It is all easy trotting on a cinder path, about half in leafy hardwoods and half on open lakeshore.

If your dog considers this ramble just a warm-up, duck through a tunnel at the south end of the lake and cross under the Southern State Parkway. The park extends for an additional two miles down a slender strip of open space to Southard Pond, a wilder cousin of Belmont Lake. You'll find miles of informal foot and bridle trails here, mixed with paved bikepaths. Preserved primarily as wetlands, these trails flood quickly in times of wet weather.

August Belmont raised more than horses on his estate. A president of the American Kennel Club for 18 years, he was well known for exhibiting smooth-coated fox terriers. Earlier, he had shown his 8-year old Gordon setter, Robin, in the first Westminster Dog Show in 1877. Two years later Robin died and is buried on the grounds.

Trail Sense: There is no map but you can go around without fear of calling the rescue dogs if you get lost.

Dog Friendliness

Dogs are allowed in the undeveloped parts of the park, which translates to the trails. No dogs permitted in the picnic areas.

Traffic

The trails are open to bikes and horses south of Sunrise Highway. For a break from the strollers and joggers around Belmont Lake the southern portion of the park is less crowded.

Canine Swimming

A grassy shelf at the south end of Belmont Lake does nicely.

Trail Time

Many hours possible.

21

Blydenburgh County Park

The Park

In 1798 cousins Caleb Smith II, Joshua Smith II and Isaac Blydenburgh went into the milling business. They constructed a 12-foot high dam across three branches of the Nissequogue River, creating the largest impoundment on the waterway. The river backed up so far into the woods that the reservoir earned the name "Stump Pond." Blydenburgh descendants operated the grist mill until 1924.

But 180-acre Stump Pond became more renowned for its trout than its flour. By the 1830s so many anglers were coming here for fat brook trout that the partners were charging a dollar a day to fish - the equivalent of an average day's pay at the time. Strict rules were crafted to regulate trout fishing on one of the largest man-made ponds on Long Island.

David Weld, a Manhattan banker, bought the estate from the Blydenburghs in 1936. The land was acquired by Suffolk County through eminent domain in 1963, although the transfer of land may have been accomplished with Weld's blessing to protect the property from suburban sprawl.

Suffolk

Phone Number
- (631) 854-3713

Website
- www.co.suffolk.ny.us/webt-emp1.cfm?dept=10&id=873

Admission Fee
- Charged during summer weekends

Park Hours
- Sunrise to sunset

Directions
- *Smithtown*; from Route 25, the West Jericho Turnpike, turn south on Brookside Drive, east of the junction with Route 25A. Make your first right on New Mill Road and follow through the neighborhoods to the park entrance at the end.

The Walks

As your dog piles out of the car, the first time visitor is confronted with a spiderweb of trail choices leading away from the parking lot. The best play is to make your way down to the shore of Stump Pond. Many of the unmarked sandy dirt paths are used by equestrians and can be cuppy and eroded but the *Lake Trail* promises surer footing.

The Blydenburgh-Weld House dominates a wide lawn that sweeps down to Stump Pond.

The bridle paths can be used to create canine hiking loops on the north shore of Stump Pond or you can continue around to the lower side of the lake on an out-and-back leg of the trail. The route is shaded by hardwoods most of the way, with a stray pine or stand of cedar thrown in. One of the last three remaining stands of old growth Atlantic white cedar can also be seen in Blydenburgh Park.

Trail Sense: Maps are available but only when the park office is open; only the *Lake Trail* is blazed. Use Stump Pond to stay oriented.

Dog Friendliness

Dogs are permitted on the beach and in the campground.

Traffic

Horses can share many of the trails and the easy-going terrain is popular with joggers.

Canine Swimming

Absolutely. There are many spots where your dog can walk into Stump Pond for some doggie aquatics - providing she doesn't mind a muddy paw or two.

Trail Time

More than one hour.

22
Cedar Island County Park

The Park

Settled on the southwest shore of Gardiners Bay in 1651, Cedar Point evolved into a bustling port for shipping farm goods, fish, and timber from Sag Harbor. The central feature of the property was its lighthouse that began opeartion in 1839.

When the light was decomissioned a century later, Wall Street lawyer Phelan Beale purchased the grounds for $2,002 with plans to turn the lighthouse into a hunting lodge for a nearby game preserve that he owned. It never happened and eventually his widow, Edith Beale, a relation of Jacqueline Kennedy Onassis and subject of the movie *Grey Gardens*, sold the lighthouse to Isabel Bradley for use as a vacation house. Suffolk County eventually purchased the property in 1967, making it part of the 607-acre Cedar Point County Park.

Suffolk County

Phone Number
- (631) 852-7620

Website
- http://www.co.suffolk.
ny.us/webtemp1.
cfm?dept=10&id=881

Admission Fee
- In season

Park Hours
- 8:00 am to sunset

Directions
- *East Hampton*; from the Montauk Highway (Route 27) pass the East Hampton Airport and make the first left onto Stephen Hands Path. Continue 2 miles, crossing Route 114 until bearing left onto Old Northwest Road. After 1.8 miles, bear right at the fork to the crossing with Alewive Brook Road. The park entrance is on the left.

The Walks

The must-do hike for dog owners at Cedar Point is the trip across the exposed sand spit to Cedar Island Lighthouse. The round-trip from the campground will cover less than two miles but can take hours depending on how much time your dog spends in the gentle waters of Northwest Harbor and Gardiners Bay. And yes, there still are cedars growing on Cedar Point.

Cedar Point is an active park with a popular campground and playground. A maze of wide dirt roads through the wooded campground offer additional hiking opportunities and you can also take off down the single-track

Northwest Path that begins its six-mile trek west in the park. On its way to Route 114, this trail passes through the Grace Estate, once owned by the shipping family, and traverses one of the largest white pine forests on Long Island.

Trail Sense: Other than the named long-distance trails passing through, the trails are not blazed but this is really not a problem. Signs along the entrance road mark the entrance to the trails.

The stony shore along Gardiners Bay will do your dog's paws no favors.

Dog Friendliness

Dogs are allowed to enjoy the trails and can stay in the campground.

Traffic

Most of the folks are in the park for camping and you will meet them on the trails in season. In winter, Cedar Point is an active wildfowl hunting area on Wednesdays through Sundays.

Canine Swimming

Your water-loving dog will want to spend as much time in the water as on the trails here.

Trail Time

A half-day of canine hiking is possible.

23
Cathedral Pines County Park

The Park

Settlement began in this area in Colonial times along the Middle Country Road, the 18th century equivalent of the Long Island Expressway. Stagecoaches stopped at Brewster's tavern and the community that grew up around the rest stop came to be known as Middle Island.

James Dayton was one of the early landowners, purchasing his home on this land in the 1790s. His sons would later expand the farm to 240 acres.

In 1968 Suffolk County acted to preserve the Prosser Pine Grove on the east side of Yaphank-Middle Island Road and a year later acquired this land to create a campground. Although it lacks the majestic pines of the Prosser grove, the new park appropriated the natural landmark for its name.

Suffolk

Phone Number
- (631) 852-5500

Website
- www.co.suffolk.ny.us/webt-emp1.cfm?dept=10&id=877

Admission Fee
- On summer weekends

Park Hours
- Sunrise to sunset

Directions
- *Middle Island*; on Yaphank-Middle Island Road, south of Route 25. From the Long Island Expressway take Exit 66 North (Sills Road). Bear left at the flashing light (Middle Island/Yaphank Road).
The park entrance is on your left just before the traffic light.

The Walks

The marquee trail through Cathedral Pines County park is a six-mile mountain bike loop that twists through the pine forest at the front of the park. If it looks like the wheeled traffic is light, this is a fine track for your dog on a sandy, pine straw surface sculpted through narrow avenues in the pines. Start the loop to your left and work counter-clockwise since this is a one-way route for the moutain bikes, heading towards you.

You can also explore the rolling hills of the park on wide sand service roads. A short nature trail is also located in the woods behind Field A. Another good place to take the dog in the park is around the large open fields in the Joseph

J. Masem Campground. Out beyond Area 9 you can hike your dog away from the camp crowds.

Trail Sense: The trailheads are well-signed and trails blazed.

Dog Friendliness
Dogs are not allowed in the playground or picnic areas but can stay in the campground.

Traffic
The park is segregated by uses and you don't have to dodge mountain bikes if you stay away from the dedicated bike trail.

Canine Swimming
None along the trails but the headwaters of Carmans River are in the park.

Trail Time
More than one mile possible.

The pines in Cathedral Pines County Park are not the giants found across the street but they do provide a pleasing backdrop for hiking with your dog.

Governor Alfred E. Smith

Sunken Meadow State Park

The Park

The park began to be assembled in 1928 during the administration of four-time Governor Alfred E. Smith. That year he became the first Roman Catholic and Irish-American to run for President as a major party nominee. After he was trounced in the election to Herbert Hoover, Smith left politics and became president of Empire State, Inc., spearheading the construction of the Empire State Building during the Great Depression.

Most of its original area of 520 acres was acquired from George and Antoinette Lamb. A large section of the beach, consisting of about 400 feet of frontage on Long Island Sound, was conveyed to the State by the Town of Smithtown in 1928. Since then the park has grown to over 1200 acres, including room for three nine-hole golf courses.

Sunken Meadow is not an old Algonquian Indian name but refers to the lowlands that separate the strip of sandy beach from the forested uplands. Access to Long Island Sound was originally by way of a quarter mile-long boardwalk erected on-stilts across the meadows and creek.

Nassau

Phone Number
- (631) 269-4333

Website
- nysparks.state.ny.us/parks/info.asp?parkID=44

Admission Fee
- Not for dog owners

Park Hours
- Sunrise to sunset

Directions
- *Northport*; dogs are not allowed to enter through the main entrance via the Sunken Meadow Parkway so you must use Old Dock Road.
From the parkway take the last exit onto Route 25A.
If you go north, turn right on Sunken Meadow Road across the park to Old Dock Road and turn left. If you go south, drive into Kings Park and turn left on Old Dock Road.

The Walks

Dogs are only allowed in the undeveloped areas of Sunken Meadows State Park and must enter the park through the servant's entrance on Old

Dock Road. The adjacent Nissequogue River State Park is also off limits to dogs so this is not a destination for long, leisurely canine hikes.

The lemonade that can be made from the lemons served up by the state include sandy, twisting trails that traverse rolling hills. There is plenty of elevation change to workout your dog and maybe a view of Long Island Sound as well.

Trail Sense: Mostly unmarked trails.

Dog Friendliness
Dogs are not allowed in picnic areas, on ballfields, on the beach, or anywhere people are playing.

Traffic
The Sunken Meadow hills are popular with joggers and cross-country runners; bikes also use these trails.

Canine Swimming
Not in the park.

Trail Time
An hour or more possible.

25

Robert Cushman Murphy County Park

The Park

In 1987, on the 100th anniversary of his birth and 14 years after his death, Suffolk County named its largest park in honor of Dr. Robert Cushman Murphy. One might lament that he was not around to enjoy such a singular honor. But don't bother. Dr. Murphy was the inspiration for the names of two mountains, Mount Murphy in the Antarctic and Murphy Wall in the South Georgia Islands, a spider, an Antarctic inlet, a plant, a fish, three species of birds, a park and a junior high school in Stony Brook, near his house in Old Field.

A fourth-generation Long Islander, Murphy was an ornithologist by training but his scientific interests were wide ranging. The founding curator of oceanic birds at the American Museum of Natural History, he wrote over 600 scientific papers in his career. He was the first scientist in modern times to call for the preservation of the Long Island pine barrens and his pioneering work on pesticides helped end the aerial spraying of the deadly DDT. All in all a life worthy of being attached to Suffolk County's first natural park.

Suffolk
Phone Number - None
Website - www.co.suffolk.ny.us/webt-emp1.cfm?dept=10&id=831
Admission Fee - None
Park Hours - Sunrise to sunset
Directions - *Manorville*; for the *Paumanok Path* take Exit 69 from the Long Island Expressway and head north on Route 25. After a mile, look for a parking area on the left. For other areas of this rambling, undeveloped park continue north and turn right on Wading River Manor Road. Turn left on Old River Road and look for a dirt access road on the right. Also, passing Old River Road, make the next left on River Road and a pull-off on the left.

The Walks

Murphy Park's 2,200 acres are dissected by rural roads that will frustrate fans of continuous trails. The only trace of development is a slice of the *Paumanok Path* across the western slab of the park that slips between Grassy

Pond and Sandy Pond. Use the network of unmarked woods roads north of the white-blazed route to create a loop among the woodland ponds.

Drive around and sample some of the other parcels to discover many rare New York species. Perhaps you'll find a mature chestnut tree - there are fewer than two dozen on Long Island. Or spy the island's most common raptor - the Red-tailed hawk. Or stands of cedars in open fields. Near the junction of River Road and Old River Road are remnant cranberry bogs.

Trail Sense: No maps or wayfinding aids at the park; only the *Paumanok Path* is blazed.

Dog Friendliness
Dogs are allowed throughout the park.
Traffic
This is not a heavily-visited park - and the absence of any signage will likely keep it that way.
Canine Swimming
If you see fishermen plying the waters of a pond it is safe to assume your dog's swimming won't be an additional disturbance. The boat ramp at Swan Lake is a good spot for canine aquatics.
Trail Time
Several hours available.

26
Manorville Hills

The Park

Manorville Hills is a 6,000-acre wilderness that is one of the largest undeveloped swaths of land on Long Island. The terrain is still testament to its glacial origins, pocked with kettle holes created by ancient chunks of melting ice. Retreating glaciers scraped out ridges and pushed up mounds. The highest of the Manorville Hills is Bald Hill that tops out at 295 feet. Managed by Suffolk County and the State of New York, this is the largest remaining remnant of the area's native pinelands.

The Walks

There are alot of reasons not to recommend the Manorville Hills as a place to bring your dog:

1) The hills are hard by the Long Island Expressway and this is the noisiest hike on Long Island. Part of the *Paumanok Path* hugs the highway so closely it is routed at the bottom the highway embankment. There are even holes in the fence for direct access to the road in case you have ever wondered what it would be like to walk your dog on the LIE.

2) The wilderness is a favorite of off-roaders and mountain bikers and you won't want to come here on a weekend without health coverage and your dog's pet insurance up to date.

3) The trails have ripped and eroded to an ankle-twisting degree in many places - your dog can disappear in some of the ruts.

4) Trash and glass on the trails are sadly common.

Suffolk

Phone Number
- None

Website
- None

Admission Fee
- None

Park Hours
- Sunrise to sunset

Directions
- *Manorville*; take Exit 70 off the Long Island Expressway and head south on Route 111. After 1.2 miles turn left on Halsey Manor Road and continue to a grassy field just short of the Expressway on the right. Park on the roadside. Another access point is another half-mile down Route 111 at Hot Water Road.

That said, there are reasons you would want to bring your dog to Manorville hills (mid-week, if possible):

1) The many dips and rolls and hill climbs in the terrain that lure the mountain bike set will thrill your dog as well, bounding to the tops in anticipation of what lies beyond.

2) The spiderweb of unmarked roads and trails make this is a great spot to try out that new GPS.

3) If you are looking for a place to disappear with your dog in the woods for a few hours, you can do it in this wilderness.

4) If you want to trade the sounds of those pesky birds for the sounds of your Ipod on the trail.

The call is yours. If you come to sample Manorville hills try to stick to Hot Water Street and Topping Path that are roomy sand roads and the widest of the bulldozer roads you encounter.

Trail Sense: The white blazes belong to the *Paumanok Path* passing through; otherwise everything is unmapped and unmarked.

Dog Friendliness
Dogs are not allowed throughout Manorville hills.
Traffic
Plenty of mountain bikes and illegal off-road vehicles.
Canine Swimming
Maybe a kettle pond will be deep enough for a quick dog paddle.
Trail Time
Many hours possible.

27
Dwarf Pine Plains Trail

The Park

There are only three places in the world where you can find communities of dwarf pines: the Shawangunk Mountains on the west side of the Hudson River, in the New Jersey Pine Barrens and here, in a four-square mile swath of Westhampton. It is unclear why these twisted pines grow little more than eight feet high but they require regular doses of fire to open pine cones while otherwise burning the trees to the ground.

Historically these lands have been little valued. The surrounding area houses industrial complexes and an airport. The military once used it as a bombing range. This property was originally acquired by Edwin Fishel and wife Ethel in 1926. They left it vacant for 70 years. Their grandchildren eventually donated the property to the State of New York. In 1993, the Long Island Pine Barrens Protection Act was passed to create and manage the Central Pine Barrens.

Suffolk

Phone Number
- None

Website
- pb.state.ny.us/

Admission Fee
- None

Park Hours
- Sunrise to sunset

Directions
- *Westhampton*; take the Sunrise Highway (Route 27) to Exit 63, heading south on Old Riverhead Road, Route 31. Trailhead and parking are at the far end of the administrative building on the left side of the road.

Your dog will feel like a giant when hiking through the dwarf pine forest.

The Walks

This fascinating slice of Long Island is easily explored on the meandering *Dwarf Pine Plains Trail* for a bit under a mile. Your dog emerges from mature woodlands into the open grounds of the pgymy pitch pines.

There is additional canine hiking to be had on unmarked trails and service roads on either side of Route 31. The little trees don't provide much shade on a hot day so have fresh drinking water available for your dog.

Trail Sense: The trail is marked by brown Carsonite directional signs but there is no trail map.

Dog Friendliness
Dogs are allowed to explore the dwarf pine forest.
Traffic
This is not a heavily-used trail.
Canine Swimming
None.
Trail Time
Less than one hour.

28
Heckscher State Park

The Park

William Nicoll, a New York City aristocrat, became the first non-native landowner in this area when he bought land from the Secatogue Indians in 1683. His mansion, Islip Grange, named after his family's ancestral estate at Northampshire, England, stood on the shoreline here, referred to as Nicolls Neck.

George C. Taylor, heir to a substantial fortune from his merchant father, pieced together a 1500-acre waterfront estate in the 1880s. It was rumored that his father's will had forbade him to marry and he lived at his manor with a common-law wife, becoming an eccentric recluse, tucked away from the prying eyes of neighbors. The local gossip ended in 1907 when the two died within days of each other.

The state park opened in 1929 following a $262,000 donation from mining magnate and philanthropist August Heckscher - over the strenuous objections from wealthy Islip neighbors. It took 25 separate appellate proceedings in every possible court from the County Court of Suffolk County to the Supreme Court of the United States to create the park. The story goes that after Governor Al Smith heard a millionaire complain that the park would be "overrun with rabble from the city" he replied, "Why, that's me," and signed the papers for the new park.

Suffolk

Phone Number
- (631) 581-2100

Website
- nysparks.state.ny.us/parks/info.asp?parkID=153

Admission Fee
- Vehicle entrance fee in season

Park Hours
- Sunrise to sunset

Directions
- *East Islip*; at the end of Heckscher Parkway from the end of the Southern Parkway or Exit 44 South from the Sunrise Highway (Route 27).

The Walks

Mostly a beach and recreation destination, dogs are allowed only on the trails behind Field 5 in Heckscher State Park. In short order you will visit a mix of marshes, open fields, a pine plantation and light woods during this low-key canine hike. It is easy trotting for your dog all the way around on wide, natural surface trails with not a hint of elevation change. While this is a worthy destination for canine hikers in the off-season, you would not want to pay state park entrance fees in the summer to use these trails.

Dogs are relegated to a small corner of the 1500-acre Heckscher State Park.

Trail Sense: There are no maps and no trail markers but there are really big red arrows posted on trees to keep dog owners in bounds.

Dog Friendliness

Dogs are not allowed on the beach, the picnic areas, the ballfields or in the campground. Dogs can also not go in any park buildings or use the walkways.

Traffic

This park buzzes with over a million visitors a year, but not many find their way to the trails behind Field 5.

Canine Swimming

If it is not busy your dog can slip into the open water at the boat ramp near the parking lot to cool off after a hike.

Trail Time

About one hour.

29

Peconic River Headwaters

The Park

European settlers first eyed the Peconic River, Long Island's longest, as a source for waterpower. Several mills sprouted along the waterway in the early 1800s. But after the Civil War the water-powered mill era on Long Island died.

In 1885 two brothers, M.H. and S.H. Woodhull, purchased land along the river from mill owner John Sweezy to start raising cranberries. Revolutionary War veteran Henry Hall had planted the first commercial cranberry beds in America in Dennis, Massachusetts in 1816 but the industry was still wide open. The Woodhull bog would soon propel Long Island into the country's third largest cranberry producer.

The cranberry era was short-lived, however. In 1967 Suffolk County began acquiring land along the Peconic River to protect it from development.

Suffolk

Phone Number
- None

Website
- None

Admission Fee
- None

Park Hours
- Sunrise to sunset

Directions
- *Riverhead*; from the Long Island Expressway take Exit 71 to Route 24 East. After one mile turn left on Pinehurst Boulevard to the end at South River Road. Turn right and continue to parking at the end of the road. The Cranberry Bog Preserve is off Riverhead-Moriches Road, one mile south of the Riverhead traffic circle.

The Walks

Hiking across these hundreds of acres of undeveloped property is a bit like exploring the woods behind your house - which you are, for somebody. Setting out, you pass abandoned furniture and assorted trash but stay with it. The sandy jeep trails roll through mixed pine and hardwood forests. Stick to the winding woods roads and ignore the many single track detours. There are no developed parking areas at the various parcels of land around the Peconic River so once you get on the trail you can expect a solitary hike with your dog.

At the Cranberry Bog Preserve your dog can explore the wetlands around Sweezy Pond on a short trail that lasts less than a mile. Water levels have changed since the cranberry-producing days but you can still stumble across remnants of the old bogs.

Trail Sense: There are no wayfinding aids here - come with a mind to explore.

Dog Friendliness
Dogs are allowed on the trails.

Traffic
More often than not your dog's adventure here will be shared with no one.

Canine Swimming
Access to the Peconic River is problematic but if you can reach it your dog will find an ideal doggie swimming pool.

Trail Time
Several hours possible.

Your dog won't object to the ungroomed nature of these trails - like examining this bullet-riddled car that looks like a Bonnie-and-Clyde getaway vehicle.

30
Indian Island
County Park

The Park

Located at the estuarine mouth of the 19-mile Peconic River, Indian Island has always been a valued area for collecting shellfish. The island was surrounded by the shallow waters of Flanders Bay where the Great Peconic Bay is squeezed by the jaws of the North and South forks.

Until the 1980s, the Peconic Bay was America's largest supplier of bay scallops, providing 28% of the nation's annual catch. In 1985 a recurring algae bloom known as Brown Tide first appeared in the bay waters. By 1996 the harvest for bay scallops was reduced from more than 500,000 pounds a year to just over 53. In 2004 New York State began the largest scallop reseeding program ever launched in the United States by tossing bug scallops into Flanders Bay from the Indian Island beach.

Suffolk

Phone Number
- (631) 852-3232

Website
- www.co.suffolk.ny.us/webt-emp1.cfm?dept=10&id=883

Admission Fee
- Yes, on summer weekends

Park Hours
- Sunrise to sunset

Directions
- *Riverhead*; take Exit 71 from the Long Island Expressway onto Route 24 South. Continue through town to Cross-River Drive (Route 105) and turn left. Park entrance is across the bridge on the right.

The Walks

This is mostly a camping and picnic park but a canine hike can still be cobbled together on the wooded paths around the campground. Unless you are staying in the campground there is no reason to bring your dog in the summer specifically to hike here but when the crowds disappear it warrants a special trip.

This is flat, easy trotting for your dog beside marshes and through light woods. The highlight will be a curving sandy beach speckled with shells and stones. In fact, Indian Island is no longer an island thanks to the creation of this sandy causeway. Your stick-fetching dog will delight in the frisky

waves the sheltered bay delivers.

Trail Sense: There is a campground map available but wayfinding on
the road grid in the self-contained park is not necessary.

Dog Friendliness

Dogs are not permitted in any picnic areas, protected bathing areas,
or sanitary facilities.

Traffic

Not many park users take advantage of the deserted campground when
the season ends.

Canine Swimming

Some of Long Island's best dog paddling is in Flanders Bay from the
Indian Island beach.

Trail Time

About one hour.

Long Island has a long history of long-distance walking.

In 1819 Stephen Pharaoh was born into one of the last of the original Montuakett Indian families living on the island. Sold into indentured service as a boy, he escaped onto a whaling ship in Sag Harbor. After he returned to live as a middle-aged man on Montauk Point stories circulated that he had joined in the California Gold Rush in 1849 and fought with the Union Army during the Civil War.

Pharaoh soon became known around eastern Long Island for his tireless walks, delivering mail for small fees. The East Hampton townsfolk called him Stephen Talkhouse as he made his rounds. Routinely he made daily round trips of up to 50 miles. As his legend grew, folks passed along the tale that he once walked from Montauk to Brooklyn in a single day.

The fame of Stephen Talkhouse attracted the notice of the greatest exhibitor of the 19th century, Phineas Taylor Barnum. For a while Barnum displayed Pharaoh as "The Last King of the Montauks," ignoring the fact that he was neither a king nor the last of the Montaukett people. Talkhouse posed for an iconic photograph with his long black hair flowing over a long jacket and brandishing his walking stick to promote his appearances. In 1879 Stephen Talkhouse was found dead, fittingly, on one of the many sandy paths he had walked so often along the Montauk bluffs. He was buried high on a hill overlooking Lake Montauk in today's Theofore Roosevelt County Park.

Stephen Talkhouse has been immortalized with a hiking trail through Hither Hills State Park and the *Paumanok Path*, named for the Algonquian name for the island, follows some of his favorite routes.

Many of Long Island's long-distance trails can be sampled in the parks described in this book. Other times they are best enjoyed with a car shuttle, if possible. Sometimes they pass through territory where dogs are allowed. For complete descriptions, maps, and up-to-date rules pertaining dogs of the long-distance trails listed below, contact the Long Island Greenbelt Trail Conference (LIGBTC - Blydenburgh County Park, *www.ligreenbelt. org*, 631-360-0141).

Long Island Greenbelt Trail

The granddaddy of the Long Island long-distance trails realized the dream of linking the Long Island Sound to the Great South Bay by footpath when it opened in 1982, four years after the founding of the LIGBTC. Running from Sunken Meadow State Park to Heckscher State Park, the is 32-mile cross island jaunt has been designated a National Recreation Trail. The route traverses the Ronkonkoma Moraine which formed during the an early part of the Wisconsin Stage of the Pleistocene Epoch (prior to about 55,000 years ago). The Ronkonkoma Moraine forms most of the low rolling hills along an east-to-west axis found below the Long Island Expressway.

Nassau-Suffolk Trail

The LIGBTC blazed a second National Recreation Trail in 1987 after three years of negotiating for old right-of-ways, public open space and private property in heavily developed Nassau County. The *Nassau-Suffolk Trail* traipses along 20 miles from Cold Spring Harbor to the Massapequa Preserve, site of the last remaining pine barrens in Nassau County. The trail is narrow singletrack along much of the course, often allowing for a parallel mountain bike trail. A connector leads to the *Walt Whitman Trail* from the Whitman Birthplace and into dog-friendly West Hills County Park.

The Pine Barrens Trail

The 1990s brought the completion of the *Pine Barrens Trail*, an ambitious routing through the heart of America's second-largest pine barrens. This 47-mile trek explores some of the wildest woodlands left on Long Island, moving southeastward from Rocky Point to Manorville.

The Paumanok Path

Alarmed by the speed of encroaching development, the East Hampton Trails Preservation Society formed in 1981. Their first formal blazed trail was the *Northwest Path* that opened in the winter of 1987-1988. This tail-friendly six-miler slices from the East Hampton-Sag Harbor Turnpike east to Cedar County Park, passing through an long-abandoned Colonial settlement. Eventually the group would blaze over 200 miles of east-end trails. Next up came the Southampton Trails Preservation Society that opened a public trail system in Red Creek Park in the early 1990s. The *Paumanok Path* seeks to link trails from the various organizations into an unbroken 120-mile chain from Rocky Point to Montauk. The *Pine Barrens Trail* covers the western half and a 45-mile string of the East Hampton group's trails have formed the easternmost 45 miles. To date, all that remains is to complete the center segments to forge Long Island's ultimate footpath.

How To Pet A Dog
Tickling tummies slowly and gently works wonders.
Never use a rubbing motion; this makes dogs bad-tempered.
A gentle tickle with the tips of the fingers is all that is necessary
to induce calm in a dog. I hate strangers who go up to dogs with their
hands held to the dog's nose, usually palm towards themselves.
How does the dog know that the hand doesn't hold something horrid?
The palm should always be shown to the dog and go straight
down to between the dog's front legs and tickle gently with
a soothing voice to accompany the action.
Very often the dog raises its back leg in a scratching movement,
it gets so much pleasure from this.
-Barbara Woodhouse

Your Dog At The Beach

It is hard to imagine any place a dog is happier than at a beach. Whether running around on the sand, jumping in the water or just lying in the sun, every dog deserves a day at the beach. But all too often dog owners stopping at a sandy stretch of beach are met with signs designed to make hearts - human and canine alike - droop: NO DOGS ON BEACH.

This sign is certainly widespread on Long Island. If you were the stretch the Long Island coastline in a single line it would cover 1,180 miles - think about a coastline from here to Chicago. Surely, there must be a place on the beach for your dog, right? Dogs are generally not allowed on Long Island Sound beaches on the North Shore but you can get your dog into the Atlantic Ocean on the South Shore. Here are some good choices, roughly heading from west to east:

Nassau Beach Park
Lido
Nassau Beach Park was welded together from three swanky private beach clubs in the 1960s. If you have seen Matt Dillon in the *Flamingo Kid* (1984) you have seen what the beach and cabanas were like. Over the years the beach became run down and "dilapidated" often equals "relaxed restrictions against dogs." Today there is a dog park off Lido Avenue at Nickerson Beach Park and Nassau Beach Park is open to dogs when the birds aren't nesting from September 15 to March 1.

Gardiner County Park
West Islip
The Beach Road in this ultra dog-friendly park leads to a sandy beach where your dog can romp in the Great South Bay. Almost any time of year she will find someone to play with in these waters.

Fire Island
Western entrance via Robert Moses Causeway
In 1857 Congress appropriated $40,000 for the construction of a 168-foot brick tower lighthouse on Fire Island, The tower stands atop a Connecticut bluestone base salvaged from the island's first tower that was built too short. The Fire Island Light was changed from a creamy yellow to its present day-mark of alternating black and white bands in August 1891. In the1980s the lighthouse was restored to its 1939 condition (when electricity was first insalled) and is still an official aid to navigation. The lighthouse beach east to the village of Kismet is open to dogs between Labor Day and mid-March.

Fire Island
Eastern entrance via William Floyd Parkway

Dogs are permitted anywhere on the wide, dune-backed sands between Labor Day and mid-March when driving is also allowed here. If you have a private boat or take a dog-friendly ferry to the interior of 32-mile Fire Island during the summer, dogs are allowed on any non-ocean, non-lifeguarded patch of sand. Dogs are never permitted on the lifeguarded beaches at Watch Hill and Sailors Haven. Additional area closures can occur at any time due to actively nesting piping plovers. If the pounding Atlantic surf is too intimidating for your dog, you can also find some sandy access along the Great South Bay. Dogs are not allowed on the beaches in the attached Robert Moses State Park on the western tip of Fire Island.

Smith Point County Park
Shirley
The park extends from the east end of the Fire Island Wilderness portion of the National Seashore to the tip of the island at Moriches Inlet. The Smith of Smith Point was William "Tangier" Smith who owned 50 miles of Long Island oceanfront in the 1600s. Most beachgoers walk to the beach through a tunnel under the dunes but dog owners need to walk past the campground entrance to the east. Wooden staircases lead over the dunes and you can take your dog all the way to Moriches Inlet. On July 17, 1996, TWA Flight 800 exploded in mid-air 14 miles offshore here, killing all 230 aboard. A granite memorial featuring the flags from the 14 countries of the victims en route from New York to Paris was dedicated in the park in 2004.

Shinnecok East County Park
Southampton
Shinnecock Inlet did not exist before September 24, 1938 when the "Great New England Hurricane" unleashed its full force on Westhampton. Still the most devastating hurricane to strike the Northeast coast, its lasting imprint here is the inlet cut through the barrier island. There is plenty of off-road activity on this beach and that means dogs can play as well.

Cooper's Beach
Southampton
This is the main beach in the village that was established in 1640 as the first English settlement in New York. Access can be problematic - and pricey - for non-residents in the summer but the sands spread far and wide in the off-season. Come in December and your dog can join in the annual Polar Bear plunge.

East Hampton Beaches
East Hampton
There are five beaches in East Hampton (only three are life-guarded) and Main Beach on Ocean Avenue is perennially ranked among the best beaches in America. Dogs and permitted on the beach before 9:00 am and and after 6:00 pm daily from the second Sunday in May through September 30. After that your dog is welcome any time.

Bridgehampton Beaches
Bridgehampton
Dogs are not allowed at any of the five town-owned beaches during the summer. If you find yourself in town between April 1 and October 1 your

dog can experience the big-breaking Atlantic Ocean waves at Peter's Pond and Gibson Beach, located east of Sagg Main Street - only before 9:00 am and after 6:00 pm and only if she stays within 150 feet of the access roads.

Amagansett Beach
Amagansett
The beach at the end of Atlantic Avenue is open for dogs all year but only before 10:00 am and after 6:00 pm between May 15 and September 15. Behind this beach is a rare double dune system that has been destroyed almost everywhere else of Long Island. If you explore the dunes with your dog be on the lookout for Fowler's Toad, America's only marine edge amphibian.

Napeague Harbor
Hither Hills State Park
Your dog is not allowed on the ocean beach at Hither Hills when the park is open but there is a sliver of sandy beach along the east shore of Napeague Harbor that is accessible from the end of Napeague Harbor Road north of Montauk Highway (Route 27). You can hike the dark brown sands north to Goff Point and Napeague Bay and the swimming is easy for your dog in the gentle waves that lap onto shore.

Napeague State Park
Promised Land
The state park stretches from the Atlantic Ocean across the neck of the South Fork to Gardiners Bay. It is totally undeveloped and looks pretty much as it did when the wetlands here were washed over by the 1938 hurricane. Access to the pristine ocean beach is by four-wheel drive vehicles only and can be closed in the summer for plover nesting. You can also try parking along the Montauk Highway (Route 27) and hike less than a half-mile to the beach on the sand road.

Ditch Plains Beach
Shadmoor State Park

This beach backed by high bluffs can be reached by hiking through the state park or from township parks from Ditch Plains Road off the Montauk Highway. Although there are large cobbles on the beach, this is the last big stretch of Atlantic Ocean sands on the eastern tip of Long Island.

Camp Hero Beach
Montauk Point
The beach below the bluffs in the old military reservation is reached by hiking down via an access road from the main parking lot. The beach is all large cobbles and the rough surf makes this primarily a beach for surfcasters and athletic swimming dogs.

Montauk Point Beaches
Montauk Point State Park
These beaches on the open waters of Block Island Sound are not wide but not crowded either, reached only by hiking trail. Although the cobbles ease

up as you move further west, these are not sunbathing beaches. Rather, the dune-backed beaches are ideal for hiking with your dog and fetching in the light waves.

Outer Beach
Theodore Roosevelt County Park
Located at the end of East Lake Road, this beach is fronted by a self-contained camper-only campground. You can also hike to this sandy/pebbly beach from the *Big Reed Nature Trail* in the park. On the west side of East Lake Road you can pull off the side of the road and toss a stick for your dog in Lake Montauk from a small sandy beach that is an East Hampton Township preserve.

Cedar Point Beach
Cedar Point County Park
Although this beach is mostly cobbles there is more than a mile of frontage on Gardiner's Bay. Stick close to water for easy hiking.

Wades Beach
Shelter Island
Most of the island between the Forks is comprised of the Mashomack Preserve that does not allow dogs. But on Midway Road, to the west of Route 114, your dog can play on 500 yards of soft sand beach on the north shore of Shelter Island Sound.

Long Beach Park
Noyack
With is shallow aqua-tinged water, this long curving beach at the foot of Noyack Bay resembles the edge of a tropical harbor. The gentle waves will entice any level of canine swimmer. Dogs are allowed on the beach year-round in designated areas, usually where the cobbles dominate the sand.

Indian Island Beach
Indian Island County Park
A crescent-shaped strip of thick sand has formed to connect Indian Island to the mainland in Flanders Bay. Some shells and stones mix with the sand and your wave-loving dog will enjoy a frothy challenge here.

Orient Point Beach
Orient
At the tip of the North Fork. Suffolk County maintains a 48-acre open space. This beach and Truman's Beach down Route 25 (East Marion residents only) played an important role during the War of 1812. A short half-mile trail leads your dog to over a mile of beach on the Long Island Sound.

Tips For Taking Your Dog To The Beach

- The majority of dogs can swim and love it, but dogs entering the water for the first time should be tested; never throw a dog into the water. Start in shallow water and call your dog's name - or try to coax him in with a treat or toy. Always keep your dog within reach.

- Another way to introduce your dog to the water is with a dog that already swims and is friendly with your dog. Let your dog follow his friend.

- If your dog begins to doggie paddle with his front legs only, lift his hind legs and help him float. He should quickly catch on and will keep his back end up.

- Swimming is a great form of exercise, but don't let your dog overdo it. He will be using new muscles and may tire quickly.

- Be careful of strong tides that are hazardous for even the best canine swimmers.

- Cool ocean water is tempting to your dog. Do not allow him to drink too much sea water. Salt in the water will make him sick. Salt and other minerals found in the ocean can damage your dog's coat so regular bathing is essential.

- Check with a lifeguard for daily water conditions - dogs are easy targets for jellyfish and sea lice.

- Dogs can get sunburned, especially short-haired dogs and ones with pink skin and white hair. Limit your dog's exposure when the sun is strong and apply sunblock to his ears and nose 30 minutes before going outside.

- If your dog is out of shape, don't encourage him to run on the sand, which is strenuous exercise and a dog that is out of shape can easily pull a tendon or ligament.

Camping With Your Dog
On Long Island

Blydenburgh County Park Campground
Smithtown
north side of Veterans Memorial Highway, opposite the H. Lee Dennison County Center in Smithtown.

RV/tent   April to October   (631) 244-7275

Cathedral Pines County Park Campground
Middle Island
on Yaphank-Middle Island Road, south of Route 25.

RV/tent   April to October   (631) 852-5502

Cedar Point County Park Campground
East Hampton
Montauk Highway east to Stephen Hands Path in East Hampton; turn north and continue to Old Northwest Road; turn right on to Northwest Road; bear left and continue to Alewive Brook Road.

RV/tent   April to October   (631) 244-7275

Cliff and Ed's Campground
Cutchogue
at 395 Schoolhouse Road off Depot Lane, north of Route 25.

RV/tent   April through November   (516) 572-8690

Cupsogue Beach County Park Campground
Westhampton
go south on Jessup Lane and cross the bridge; turn right onto Dune Road; follow Dune Road to its western terminus in Westhampton Beach.

RV only   April to October   (631) 852-8111

Eastern Long Island Kampgrounds
Greenport
at the end of Queens Street, south of Route 25.

RV/tent   early May to early November   (631) 477-0022

Indian Island County Park Campground
Riverhead
on Cross-River Drive (Route 105), north of Route 24.
RV/tent   **April to October**   **(631) 244-7275**

Sears Bellows County Park Campground
Hampton Bays
on Sears Bellows Road off Route 24 from Exit 65 North of the Sunrise Highway.
RV/tent   **April to October**   **(631) 244-7275**

Shinnecock East County Park Campground
East Hampton
go south on Halsey Neck Lane off Montauk Highway to Dune Road; make a right turn onto Dune Road and head west to the park entrance.
RV only   **open year-round**   **(631) 852-8899**
                                                            in-season
                                                            (631) 852-8290
                                                            off-season

Smith Point County Park Campground
Shirley
*take William Floyd Parkway from Long Island Expressway, Exit 68 South
to its southern terminus at Fire Island.*
RV only   **April to October**   **(631) 244-7275**

Southaven County Park Campground
Brookhaven
*on Victory Avenue off William Floyd Parkway north of Sunrise Highway,
Exit 58.*
RV/tent   **April to October**   **(631) 854-1418**

Theodore Roosevelt County Park Campground
Montauk
at end of East Lake Drive off Montauk Highway, east of Montauk village.
RV only   **April to October**   **(631) 852-7879**

Tips For Taking Your Dog To The Dog Park

🐾 Keep an eye on your dog and a leash in hand. Situations can change quickly in a dog park.

🐾 Keep puppies younger than 4 months at home until they have all necessary innoculations to allow them to play safely with other dogs. Make certain that your older dog is current on shots and has a valid license.

🐾 ALWAYS clean up after your dog. Failure to pick up your dog's poop is the quickest way to spoil a dog park for everyone.

- If your dog begins to play too rough, don't take time to sort out blame - leash the dog and leave immediately.

- Leave your female dog at home if she is in heat.

- Don't volunteer to bring all the dogs in the neighborhood with you when you go. Don't bring any more dogs than you can supervise comfortably.

- Observe and follow all posted regulations at the dog park.

- HAVE AS MUCH FUN AS YOUR DOG

How To Follow A Trail

The more you take your dog hiking, the more you are exposed to the different ways parks mark their trails. The best parks will provide you with a mapboard to study, a trail map to take along, brief trail descriptions - including distances - of what to expect, well-marked trails, and junction signs.

Most parks won't give you all that - you'll get some items from the menu or maybe none at all. The more you hike with your dog the more you will find yourself making a wrong turn somewhere. Even when you are really paying attention it is surprisingly easy to miss a turn out in the woods. Unless you are looking for a true wilderness experience with compass and wayfinding aides you are not going to want to go into the woods unless you have a trail map. A trail map, even if it is a bit sketchy, will keep you from getting lost if you find the trails not enthusiastically marked.

Often a printed map isn't available but one is posted at the trailhead. Grab a piece of scrap paper from your car and sketch a rudimentary map before heading out rather than rely on your memory. Uut in the woods things can turn confusing.

Once on the trail you will be following colored blazes painted on trees. The very best trails will be blazed often enough that you will see the next blaze immediately after passing the previous one. This is seldom the case, however. Trees with blazes fall over, paint fades from trails that are not maintained or blazes are just applied sparingly. This is why it is important to start with a map - to reinforce your confidence on poorly marked trails.

Big parks can have an elaborate trail system with many colored trails - the most I have ever seen is 23 trails all blazed in different solid or multi colors. The same path may be used by several trails so pay attention. On many long-distance, multi-day trails (the *Paumanok Path*, for instance) the main trail is marked in white and EVERY side trail is blazed in blue.

Some parks don't blaze their trails at all - they rely on signposts at trail junctions to guide you here and there. Again, a map is a must at these parks since you don't want to come to a junction where a signpost has disappeared or been stolen by vandals. Incidentally, trail junctions at parks that don't use signs are indicated by two blazes one on top of the other. The higher of the two blazes is offset in the direction you want to go, ie., if the upper blaze is a bit further left than the bottom, turn left. On the best-marked trails you will also sometimes find three blazes in the shape of a triangle - that marks the end of a trail. Congratulations - you made it back, and hopefully you didn't have to rely on your dog's nose.

Is Your Dog Overheating?

You may have noticed your dog panting alot in summer. But just because it is hot and your dog is panting doesn't mean he is in trouble on the trail. Aside from a few, mostly useless, sweat glands on his feet your dog doesn't have any sweat glands and must rely exclusively on panting to breathe off excess heat. This is obviously not very efficient and makes your dog more susceptible to heatstroke much quicker than we are in hot summer weather.

Heatstroke is nearly always preventable - it's biggest enemy is common sense. Don't plan long, tough hikes in the heat of the day. Leave the big hikes with your older dog for cooler weather. If you are hiking with your dog in summer, don't leave the trailhead without an inexhaustible supply of drinking water. On the trail with your dog - in any weather, but especially in the summer - if he drops behind you, stop and take a break. If you have a short-nosed breed like a Boxer or a double-coated breed like a German Shepherd, heat will be even more of a factor on a hike.

It can be difficult to differentiate between normal heavy panting and the rapid panting that is a sign of heatstroke. If your dog's eyes become glassy or his gums turn bright red, take action immediately. Cool down your dog as fast as possible. Use cool water - icy water can cause too drastic a body temperature change - applied directly or with soaked towels to the head, neck, chest and abdomen. Take you time and sit in the shade awhile - don't rush your dog back on the trail.

Most times heatstroke is an isolated incident and your recovered dog will not have any lasting problems. You may want to take him to the vet for a check-up just to be on the safe side, however.

"Dogs' lives are too short. Their only fault, really."
-Agnes Sligh Turnbull

Your Dog And Skunks

Your dog won't meet many skunks on the trail since they are active by night and reclusive by day. Your dog is more likely to encounter a skunk in your own back yard or near a garbage pile in a campground. What should you do if your dog comes out the loser in a scrape with this weasel?

First of all, time is not on your side. Do your best to keep the spray wet before you actually deal with it. If you wake up in the morning and your dog has been skunked during the night and the spray is dry you will have a dickens of a time ridding your dog of the odor. Every time he gets wet for the next two years you may still detect a whiff of that night with the skunk.

The story you may have heard is to attack the stench with tomato juice. That may mask the smell for an hour but otherwise it won't do anything beyond turning your dog red. To best neutralize a skunk's spray try the following mixture:

* 1 quart (or liter) of 3% Hydrogen Peroxide, H2O2.
* 1/4 cup (50 ml.) of Baking Soda
* 1 teaspoon (5 ml.) of Liquid Soap

The Hydrogen Peroxide and baking soda combine to neutralize the smell; the soap breaks up the oils in the skunk spray, allowing the other ingredients to do their work. Wash your dog in the solution and let it sit about ten minutes before rinsing. You still may detect a whisp of skunk but it will be better.

Unfortunately you cannot pre-mix this solution and store it in anticipation of a skunk problem - if kept bottled up it will explode. Also, if your Hyrdrogen Peroxide has been sitting on the shelf for awhile it may have already turned to water so you may have to run out and get a fresh bottle.

Skunks can be a particularly nasty varmint. If you do run into a skunk on the trail during the day or see one that is agressive it could well be rabid. The occurrence of rabid skunks appears highest from February to May, when they breed and give birth to their young.

Your Dog's Tough Feet

You are out on a hike with tough hiking boots and after a long day on a your feet are screaming at you. Did you ever wonder how your bare-footed dog manages out there?

A dog's foot pads are composed of several layers of keratin, a harder form of skin cells. You can actually build up the toughness of your dog's pads. If you have a big hike planned you can treat your dog's pads in the weeks before with a product called Pad-Tough. It is a botanical product with aloe and comfrey. It comes in a spray form. Simply coat your dog's paw pads liberally before any rigorous activity. A four-ounce bottle cost s between $10 and $15.

Check your dog's pads during and after a long hike. Dogs are stoic and may not give a reaction to splinters and the like. If you discover a tough-to-get object embedded in your dog's paws try using a piece of sticky tape to pull it out or, if your dog is resting, put a drop of white glue on the paw. When it dries, peel it off and the splinter will pull right out.

In the winter dogs can get frostbite on unprotected feet in very cold weather - frostbite can also affect ears and tails. And when it is cold and wet always take a moment to dry and clean your dog's paws to help avoid tiny cuts and cracked footpads. The rock salt that is used to melt ice on paved surfaces may also irritate footpads which is another reason to keep your dog's paws clean.

Most dogs love to romp in the snow. Before the drifts pile up clip the hair around your dog's pawpads to ease snow removal and help prevent ice balls from forming. You don't want to use powerful hot-air dryers to melt those little ice balls because you can burn your dog's skin.

"They are superior to human beings as companions. They do not quarrel or argue with you. They never talk about themselves but listen to you while you talk about yourself, and keep an appearance of being interested in the conversation."
-Jerome K. Jerome

How To Give
The Perfect Dog Bath

Most pet owners do not think twice about spending big dollars to buy their dog premium dog food, the best health care or even blissful days at a doggie day care facility. Most pet owners also don't think twice when it's time to give Bowser a bath. Grab the Head and Shoulders and fire up the backyard garden hose.

But a proper dog bath is vital to maintaining your pet's vigorous good health. The skin is the body's largest organ and a perfect dog bath is key to stimulating blood circulation and keeping the skin healthy. Improper bathing can cause a matted condition in the coat which is uncomfortable to your dog.

The first step in the perfect dog bath is a good brushing. For short-haired dogs brush in a circular motion with a curry comb made of rubber with teeth cut into the edges. It will pull the dead coat out. Slicker brushes will take out the dead undercoat. Start on the legs and hold the outer hair so that you can brush from the skin outward. If it is not removed, the coat will easily mat. Use this technique all over the dog - legs, body and tail. Dogs resent the tail being brushed so save it for last. For fine-haired dogs use a natural bristle brush. Moisten the area to be worked with a good coat conditioner.

For long-haired dogs use a pin brush if the coat is not tangled, a slicker brush if the coat is tangled. Start at the legs, again brushing from the skin out and brushing only a few hairs at a time. The secret to thorough brushing is to brush only a few hairs at a time. Check each area with a comb; if the comb goes through without stress continue all the way up to the middle of the dog's back. Go to the loin area and to the back legs; then move to each side of the back of the dog.

"Dog. A kind of additional or subsidiary Deity
designed to catch the overflow and surplus
of the world's worship."
-Ambrose Bierce

You are now ready to wash. Never use human shampoos to wash your dog. Dog shampoos are specially formulated to match the pH level of a dog's skin. Human shampoos can strip a dog's coat of essential oils.

The right way to bathe a dog is determined by the texture and length of the coat. Short-haired dogs are washed with a vigorous circular motion which will pull out the dirt. On dogs with a medium-length coast, use a back-and-forth motion. As the hair gets longer, go only in the direction the hair grows.

Step 1.
Rinse the dog completely.

Step 2.
Apply the shampoo along the back; do the same with the belly, legs and tail. Don't worry about building lather - lather doesn't clean your dog and too much is difficult to wash out.

Step 3.
Rinse the coat with one hand to run water on the dog and the other hand in a kneading fashion to work the soap out. Make certain all the soap is out as dried soap will dull a coat and cause skin problems.

Step 4.
Before towel-drying, squeeze as much water out of the coat as possible by pulling the hair straight out and squeezing at the same time.

Step 5.
Use a washcloth to clean the dog's face and avoid getting water in his ears. Moisture inside the ears provides the conditions for fungus infections.

Step 6.
Towel dry your dog and use a hand-held hair dryer on thick-coated dogs but never use a human hair dryer as they run too hot and can burn the dog and damage the coat.

Voila! A clean, healthy dog.

The Other End Of The Leash

Leash laws are like speed limits - everyone seems to have a private interpretation of their validity. Some dog owners never go outside with an unleashed dog; others treat the laws as suggestions or disregard them completely. It is not the purpose of this book to tell dog owners where to go to evade the leash laws or reveal the parks where rangers will look the other way at an unleashed dog. Nor is it the business of this book to preach vigilant adherence to the leash laws. Nothing written in a book is going to change people's behavior with regard to leash laws. So this will be the last time leash laws are mentioned, save occasionally when we point out the parks where dogs are welcomed off leash.

Index to Parks and Open Spaces...

Tribute To The Dog

As a young lawyer, 19th century Senator George Graham Vest of Missouri, addressed the jury on behalf of his client, suing a neighbor who had killed his dog. Vest's speech has come to be known as "Tribute to the Dog."

The best friend a man has in the world may turn against him and become his enemy. His son or daughter that he has reared with loving care may prove ungrateful. Those who are nearest and dearest to us, those whom we trust with our happiness and our good name may become traitors to their faith. The money that a man has, he may lose. It flies away from him, perhaps when he needs it most. A man's reputation may be sacrificed in a moment of ill-considered action. The people who are prone to fall on their knees to do us honor when success is with us may be the first to throw the stone of malice when failure settles its cloud upon our heads.

The one absolutely unselfish friend that man can have in this selfish world, the one that never deserts him, the one that never proves ungrateful or treacherous is his dog. A man's dog stands by him in prosperity and in poverty, in health and in sickness. He will sleep on the cold ground, where the wintry winds blow and the snow drives fiercely, if only he may be near his master's side. He will kiss the hand that has no food to offer; he will lick the wounds and sores that come in an encounter with the roughness of the world. He guards the sleep of his pauper master as if he were a prince. When all other friends desert, he remains. When riches take wings, and reputation falls to pieces, he is as constant in his love as the sun in its journey through the heavens.

If fortune drives the master forth an outcast in the world, friendless and homeless, the faithful dog asks no higher privilege than that of accompanying him, to guard him against danger, to fight against his enemies. And when the last scene of all comes, and death takes his master in its embrace and his body is laid away in the cold ground, no matter if all other friends pursue their way, there by the graveside will the noble dog be found, his head between his paws, his eyes sad, but open in alert watchfulness, faithful and true even in death.

About The Author

Doug Gelbert is the author of 35 books, including 17 on hiking with your dog. He formed Cruden Bay Books in 1995 to publish centennial history books of golf & country clubs (Cruden Bay is a golf course in northeast Scotland). Today the company specializes in producing local guides to hiking with your dog with more than 20 in print. Cruden Bay Books also publishes the acclaimed national guide to hiking with your dog, THE CANINE HIKER'S BIBLE. Gelbert also leads hiking tours for people and their dogs between New York and Maryland. For more information visit the website, *www.hikewithyourdog.com.*

DOGGIN' THE MID-ATLANTIC: *400 Tail-Friendly Parks To Hike With Your Dog In New Jersey, Pennsylvania, Delaware, Maryland and Northern Virginia* - $18.95
DOGGIN' THE POCONOS: *The 33 Best Places To Hike With Your Dog In Pennsylvania's Northeast Mountains* - $9.95
DOGGIN' THE BERKSHIRES: *The 33 Best Places To Hike With Your Dog In Western Massachusetts* - $9.95
DOGGIN' NORTHERN VIRGINIA: *The 50 Best Places To Hike With Your Dog In NOVA* - $9.95
DOGGIN' DELAWARE: *The 40 Best Places To Hike With Your Dog In The First State* - $9.95
DOGGIN' MARYLAND: *The 100 Best Places To Hike With Your Dog In The Free State* - $12.95
DOGGIN' JERSEY: *The 100 Best Places To Hike With Your Dog In The Garden State* - $12.95
DOGGIN' RHODE ISLAND: *The 25 Best Places To Hike With Your Dog In The Ocean State* - $7.95
DOGGIN' THE FINGER LAKES: *The 50 Best Places To Hike With Your Dog* - $12.95
DOGGIN' CONNECTICUT: *The 57 Best Places To Hike With Your Dog In The Nutmeg State* - $12.95
DOGGIN' LONG ISLAND: *The 30 Best Places To Hike With Your Dog In New York's Playground* - $9.95
DOGGIN' THE TIDEWATER: *The 33 Best Places To Hike With Your Dog from the Northern Neck to Virginia Beach* - $9.95
DOGGIN' NORTHWEST FLORIDA: *The 50 Best Places To Hike With Your Dog in the Panhandle* - $12.95
DOGGIN' THE CAROLINA COASTS: *The 50 Best Places To Hike With Your Dog Along The North Carolina And South Carolina Shores* - $11.95
DOGGIN' AMERICA'S BEACHES: *A Traveler's Guide To Dog-Friendly Beaches - (and those that aren't)* - $12.95
THE CANINE HIKER'S BIBLE - $19.95
A Bark In The Park: The 55 Best Places To Hike With Your Dog In The Philadelphia Region - $12.95
A Bark In The Park: The 50 Best Places To Hike With Your Dog In The Baltimore Region - $12.95
A Bark In The Park: The 37 Best Places To Hike With Your Dog In Pennsylvania Dutch Country - $9.95

45510858R00066

Made in the USA
Middletown, DE
06 July 2017